I Am Encouraged!
You Be Encouraged, Too!

A 90-Day Devotional to Move from Pain to Power

BUNNY DEBARGE

ISBN 979-8-9882366-3-4

Cover Design by J. D. Williams

PRINTED IN THE UNITED STATES OF AMERICA
First edition, 2023

Dream Music, LLC
Detroit, Michigan

Author Website:
www.officialbunnydebarge.com

Dedication

To my amazing followers on social media who inspired me to compile

my words of encouragement into a book.

He Has Been Waiting on You

(A Prophetic Poem)

It is going to be alright!

The Father has your attention now; that's a good thing.

Now keep your attention right there.

Stay humble and watch him, Beloved.

Yield to the Spirit. He's amazing.

Let him breathe on your life like only he can.

He has been waiting on you.

Table of Contents

Preface

I am extremely honored to share these words of healing. This book has been prayerfully written to minister to you. Throughout the writing process, the Holy Spirit ministered to me as well. Every word has been saturated in prayer.

Each devotional includes between two (2) and five(5) scriptures to meditate upon for the day. At times, I have selected scriptures from different translations to open up a broader meaning of the text. I encourage you to engage and connect with the content. Pay close attention to the parts on soul healing and joy. As the wounds in your soul are healed, you will see healing manifest in other areas of your life. I pray that the words of this book leap off the pages into your spirit. Find your own way to pull the written words into your heart and live them out in a very practical manner. Expect the Holy Spirit to speak to you personally beyond what I have shared.

I love you and have prayed for you. I am so excited about the good life God has in store for you.

Love,
Bunny DeBarge
2023

Part 1
Love

The Father's Loving Care

Father, I thank you for holding me together each and every day.

Whenever I have needed you, you've been right here for me.

Whenever I've called on your name,

I know that you've heard my cry.

Thank you for your faithfulness even through the rough times.

Even when I was so consumed with the problems in my life,

and I could not utter a word,

You, Father, heard my silent cry; you read my mind.

To you alone be the glory.

Your presence is the safest place I can be.

I praise you, Lord, for you are the God of Mercy and the God of

Grace.

The one who knows my thoughts, my feelings,

and sees my deepest desires.

I am grateful to be able to call on your name.

Thank you Jesus for loving and caring for me.

Bunny DeBarge

Day 1

Receive His Love

John 13:34-35 MSG

*Let me give you a new command: Love one another. In the same way I
loved you, you love one another. This is how everyone will recognize that
you are my disciples—when they see the love
you have for each other.*

Ephesians 3:17-19 NIV

*17 so that Christ may dwell in your hearts through faith. And I pray
that you, being rooted and established in love,
18 may have power, together with all the Lord's holy people, to grasp
how wide and long and high and deep is the love of Christ,
19 and to know this love that surpasses knowledge—that you may be
filled to the measure of all the fullness of God.*

Grace and Peace, Beloved!

The love of Jesus far surpasses our natural understanding. It is not an "any old kind of love" that we throw around "any old kind of way." No, this love is wide, long, high, and deep (Ephesians 3:18 NIV). It is so vast that every facet of our life in Christ is based upon his love. Once we understand the immensity of God's love for us, we will never accept defeat.

As I reflect on my own life, I know I did not get everything right. I am so grateful to Jesus for looking past my faults and continuing to do so. He understands me, my mishaps, and will never turn his back on me.

He loves you, Beloved, exactly the same. His grace covers our sin. In like manner, we are to love our sisters and brothers. Jesus is our example. Jesus did not leave us without the help we need to love others. The Holy Spirit is here to help us. We can do it – not in our own strength – but with the Holy Spirit's help. Demonstrating that type of love is a testament to the world that we belong to him.

Today's Prayer:

Father, I receive your extravagant love today. You love me so much that you sent your son Jesus to redeem me back to you. Jesus loves me so comprehensively that he died for me. I am in awe of your love for me. I receive it freely and unconditionally; I give it freely and unconditionally. Holy Spirit, thank you for helping me to love like you. In the mighty name of Jesus, I pray. Amen!

I am encouraged! You be encouraged, too!

Day 2

Never Separated From His Love

Romans 8:38-39 KJV

38 For I am persuaded, that neither death, nor life, nor angels, nor principalities,

nor powers, nor things present, nor things to come,

39 Nor height, nor depth, nor any other creature, shall be able to separate us from the love of God, which is in Christ Jesus our Lord.

Psalm 139:7 NLT

I can never escape from your Spirit! I can never get away from your presence!

Grace and Peace, Beloved!

Regardless of what we go through, nothing will ever separate us from the love of God! His love is expansive; it reaches far and wide. It permeates our inner most being and dwells on the inside of us. We are carriers of his love; therefore, we can never be without it. Let us extend our roots more deeply in his presence today. We revel in the beauty of his love.

If you believe God loves you deeply and unconditionally, thank him for it. Have faith in the power of his love.

Today's Prayer:

Father, thank you for loving me! I am wrapped, swaddled, and enveloped in your unfailing love. I declare that the enemy's lies shall not be my reality but that your word alone prevails! Your will stands firmly in my life. Every ill-spoken word against me is nullified and void! I reject, cancel, and unsubscribe to satan's schemes and tactics. I am loved by you, and that is all that matters. In the mighty name of Jesus, I pray! Amen.

I am encouraged! You be encouraged, too!

Day 3

Love Covers Our Faults

Matthew 18:12-13 KJV

12 How think ye? if a man have an hundred sheep, and one of them be gone astray, doth he not leave the ninety and nine, and goeth into the mountains, and seeketh that which is gone astray?
13 And if so be that he find it, verily I say unto you, he rejoiceth more of that sheep, than of the ninety and nine which went not astray.

Ephesians 4:30 KJV

And grieve not the holy Spirit of God, whereby ye are sealed unto the day of redemption.

Ezekiel 34:16 KJV

I will seek that which was lost, and bring again that which was driven away, and will bind up that which was broken, and will strengthen that which was sick:
but I will destroy the fat and the strong;
I will feed them with judgment.

Grace and Peace, Beloved!

Let us thank God for his undying love for us! Even if we walk away from him, Beloved, (and we all have been there) he still loves us. He is still faithful to open his arms in love. Consider Adam and Eve, the first transgressors. In his infinite wisdom, God had a plan to redeem every human being back to him. He stands outside of time to ensure his master plan for mankind is completed. That master plan includes us.

I am so grateful that he looks beyond our faults and sees our needs. We can take the test again. He still calls us to repent and to come back to him. It is his grace that continuously sustains us. His love is always with us.

Today's Prayer:

Thank you, Father, for your everlasting mercy. Oh, how merciful you are! Despite my shortcomings, the Holy Spirit has sealed me for you until the very day that Jesus returns. I love how you love me. Your strong, steadfast arms have protected me from danger, both seen and unseen. You uphold me with your righteous hand. I am sustained by you. Thank you for helping me live a life that pleases you. In the mighty name of Jesus, I pray! Amen.

I am encouraged! You be encouraged, too!

Day 4
Bondage-Breaking Love

Isaiah 1:18 KJV

Come now, and let us reason together, saith the Lord: though your sins be as scarlet, they shall be as white as snow; though they be red like crimson, they shall be as wool.

Romans 5:20 TPT

So then, the law was introduced into God's plan to bring the reality of human sinfulness out of hiding. And yet, wherever sin increased, there was more than enough of God's grace to triumph all the more!

Isaiah 43:25 NLT

I—yes, I alone—will blot out your sins for my own sake and will never think of them again.

Micah 7:18 NIV

Who is a God like you, who pardons sin and forgives the transgression of the remnant of his inheritance? You do not stay angry forever but delight to show mercy.

Psalm 36:7 AMP

How precious is Your lovingkindness, O God! The children of men take refuge in the shadow of Your wings.

Grace and Peace, Beloved!

Many people stay away from God because they have become entangled in habits or patterns that they can not break. Reflecting on my own journey, I was told God does not hear you when you are in that place. That viewpoint is so far from the truth, Beloved! The Lord delights in showing mercy. He will meet you right where you are.

I dare you to respond to his everlasting love and call him. Simply say, "Lord, if you are who you say you are, come see about me." Don't wait until you quit smoking, using drugs, watching pornography, or taking part in any other harmful behaviors. Believe me, those vices are no barrier to his love.

Don't get it twisted; you need God's help! None of us will ever be enough on our own. Your flesh likes what you are doing and will always try to satisfy itself. So don't put the cart before the horse. Give yourself to Jesus. Turn your life over to him and let him be who he is, the Savior! The more you seek him, the more you will find a life that is worth living. Again, you can't do it by yourself. Jesus will take care of everything as you let the Spirit of God conform you into his image. Yield, Beloved! Don't work from the outside in. It will never happen. Let Him transform you from the inside out!

If you know of someone who can benefit from this message on bondage-breaking love, please feel free to pray this prayer with them.

Today's Prayer:

Jesus, if you are who you say you are, come see about me. I cannot break these habits on my own. I need your help. Thank you for loving me unconditionally. In the mighty name of Jesus, I pray! Amen.

I am encouraged! You be encouraged, too!

Day 5

Seeds of Love, Kindness, and Financial Generosity

2 Corinthians 9:6-8 NIV

*6 Remember this: Whoever sows sparingly will also reap sparingly,
and whoever sows generously will also reap generously.
7 Each of you should give what you have decided in your heart to
give, not reluctantly or under compulsion,
for God loves a cheerful giver.
8 And God is able to bless you abundantly, so that in all things at all
times, having all that you need,
you will abound in every good work.*

Psalm 112:5 VOICE

*Good comes to all who are gracious and share freely; they conduct
their affairs with sound judgment.*

Ephesians 5:2 KJV

*And walk in love, as Christ also hath loved us,
and hath given himself for us an offering and a sacrifice to God for a
sweetsmelling savour.*

Grace and Peace, Beloved!

God commands us to love. Period. He has already demonstrated how we are to love. His love is extravagant, unfailing, endless, inexhaustible, purifying, sanctifying, and complete. We know in our spirits how to love because the Father has given all to reconcile us to him. The love that we have received freely, we freely give to others. That love may take on different presentations – giving to those in need, sharing a kind word with someone who is discouraged, sowing financially into worthy causes, praying for our family members, healing the sick, raising the dead, and most importantly, introducing someone to the God who loved us first.

Be intentional in your love, bodacious in your kindness, and enthusiastic in your giving! It's all good, Beloved. Plant those seeds from your heart as the Holy Spirit leads! The supernatural harvest on those seeds is inevitable.

Today's Prayer:

Father, I thank you, that you have given me a heart to love and give. When I feel it is difficult to love, I remember your love for me. I do not need to strain myself to love; I simply activate your love. Thank you for giving me seed to sow. I yield to you regarding my giving. Show me the people whom you have called me to serve. Thank you, Father, for answered prayer. In the mighty name of Jesus, I pray! Amen.

I am encouraged! You be encouraged, too!

Part 2
God's Character

Day 6

God's Sovereignty

Psalm 115:3 NIV

Our God is in heaven; he does whatever pleases him.

Jude 25 KJV

To the only wise God our Saviour, be glory and majesty,
dominion and power, both now and ever. Amen.

Hebrews 4:13 NIV

Nothing in all creation is hidden from God's sight. Everything is
uncovered and laid bare before the eyes of him
to whom we must give account.

Grace and Peace, Beloved!

God is sovereign and is in every detail of our lives. Think about it. He knows every hair on our heads and when they fall out. He knows every sparrow that falls from the tree. He is all-knowing, all-seeing, and all-wise. Nothing is hidden from him. This God can take what was meant for evil and work it for good! He has the final word on every matter. We may as well consult him first. What a mighty God we serve!

Give all of your concerns to him. He knows how to make your enemies serve you and help you to move forward on his righteous path.

Today's Prayer:

Father, I am so glad that you know all things about me. Even when I have no earthly person to whom I can turn, you already know my thoughts. I am grateful that your throne of grace is always open. You always welcome me. Help me today to trust you with the tiny details of my life - those things that may seem insignificant to some but are important to me. I trust you forever. In the mighty name of Jesus, I pray! Amen.

I am encouraged! You be encouraged, too!

Day 7

The Life-Giver

John 10:10 KJV

*The thief cometh not, but for to steal, and to kill,
and to destroy: I am come that they might have life,
and that they might have it more abundantly.*

John 8:12 KJV

*Then spake Jesus again unto them, saying, I am the light of the world:
he that followeth me shall not walk in darkness, but shall have the light of
life.*

John 4:14 KJV

*But whosoever drinketh of the water that I shall give him shall never
thirst; but the water that I shall give him shall be in him
a well of water springing up into everlasting life.*

Grace and Peace, Beloved!

Remember God is our source, and I am not talking about money only. He is our source for life. He is our source for peace, hope, stability, strength, guidance, and deliverance. He has already provided all that we need to sustain us for an abundant life that honors him. He came to give us abundant life! Just like sunlight, he is the life-giver and the light. Just like water, he quenches our thirst. He fills us with the Holy Spirit so that rivers of living water flow from deep within our souls. He is also the bread of life; we who hunger for him are filled to satisfaction. Everything that we need is in him!

As I write these words, I draw from the life-giver. I go into my re-created spirit and withdraw all that is needed to thrive and prosper.

Today's Prayer:

Father, I thank you for being my source. I lack nothing. You own this world and all that is in it. I am your child with access to all that you have. I thank you for your divine supply of all that I need to lead a robust life that honors you. Continue to strengthen and encourage me. Lead me on your righteous path, for I can do nothing without you. Allow others to see your love through me. You are love, and I am rooted and grounded in you. In the mighty name of Jesus, I pray! Amen.

I am encouraged! You be encouraged, too!

Day 8

Always

Matthew 28:19-20 KJV

*19 Go ye therefore, and teach all nations, baptizing them in the name
of the Father,and of the Son, and of the Holy Ghost:
20 Teaching them to observe all things whatsoever I have
commanded you: and, lo,
I am with you always, even unto the end of the world. Amen.*

1 Corinthians 13:6-7 NIV

*6 Love does not delight in evil but rejoices with the truth.
7 It always protects, always trusts, always hopes, always perseveres.*

Revelation 1:8 KJV

*I am Alpha and Omega, the beginning and the ending,
saith the Lord, which is, and which was, and which is to come, the
Almighty.*

Grace and Peace, Beloved!

The supreme love of God is always. His love is perfect, pure, trustworthy, right, and everlasting. It is a love that we can depend on. It is safe, secure, and stable. In unstable times, God is our stability. He is always with us, always helping us, always providing for us, always keeping us, always strengthening us, and always providing for us. He was, and is, and is to come. He is eternal.

Take some time to ponder on the magnitude of "always." There is no time when God has been absent from your life, your circumstances, your disillusionment, your joy, your happy times, or any other time that you can name. He will never be an absentee father. You can withstand anything because he is always there.

Today's Prayer:

Holy Spirit, I rely on you to guide me today as you promised you would. Lead me today through perfect prayers as I pray in heaven's language and praise you throughout this day. Thank you for your presence and for the mind to know that you are "always" there! In the mighty name of Jesus, I pray! Amen.

I am encouraged! You be encouraged, too!

Day 9

Promise Keeper

Psalm 37:4 KJV

Delight thyself also in the Lord:
and he shall give thee the desires of thine heart.

2 Corinthians 1:20 KJV

For all the promises of God in him are yea, and in him Amen,
unto the glory of God by us.

2 Peter 1:4 NLT

And because of his glory and excellence, he has given us great and
precious promises. These are the promises that enable you to share his
divine nature and escape the world's corruption caused by human desires.

Grace and Peace, Beloved!

Most of us have heard someone say, "Promises, promises," in a flippant way. The tone alone indicates that the speaker does not believe the person who made the promise because of a pattern of not keeping his word. Not so with our Lord. He always keeps his word. We have great and precious promises from the Promise Keeper. We trust him to fulfill them all.

In Psalms, David encourages us to delight ourselves in the Lord. According to the Merriam-Webster online dictionary, the verb form of delight is "to take great pleasure (Merriam-Webster, n.d.)." As we enjoy the Lord and his company, we rest assured that he grants our desires.

Commit your ways to the Lord, Beloved. Trust in him, and he will act. Leaning on him for all things is a recipe for good living.

Today's Prayer:

Thank you, heavenly Father, for the promised blessings that come with just knowing you. You are transforming me into your exact image. As I am blessed, I will be a blessing to others. Your love is contagious! In the mighty name of Jesus, I pray! Amen.

I am encouraged! You be encouraged, too!

Day 10

Truth Teller

Numbers 23:19 KJV

God is not a man, that he should lie; neither the son of man, that he should repent: hath he said, and shall he not do it? or hath he spoken, and shall he not make it good?

Hebrews 6:13, 18 KJV

13 For when God made promise to Abraham, because he could swear by no greater, he sware by himself,

18 That by two immutable things, in which it was impossible for God to lie, we might have a strong consolation, who have fled for refuge to lay hold upon the hope set before us:

John 14:6 KJV

Jesus saith unto him, I am the way, the truth, and the life: no man cometh unto the Father, but by me.

Grace and Peace, Beloved!

We can trust our Father absolutely because he cannot lie. Understand the significance of the word "cannot." On the contrary, man has the capacity to lie, although in good faith he may commit to put away lying. Our Father cannot lie because it is not in his character. His core is truth. The father of lies is satan; know that every time satan speaks, lies come forth. Every time our good Father speaks, it is truth. That principle undergirds our ability to trust him in everything.

Take your trust to the next level, Beloved!

Today's Prayer:

Father, I thank you for always speaking truth to me. I can count on you. Cleanse my mind of experiences where man has lied to me. Help me to disconnect from those memories. Truthfulness is your character and I follow your example. In the mighty name of Jesus, I pray! Amen.

I am encouraged! You be encouraged, too!

Day 11

His Life-Changing Presence

Luke 19:8-10 TPT

8 Zacchaeus was amazed over his gracious visit to his home and
joyously welcomed Jesus.
Zacchaeus stood in front of the Lord and said, "Half of all that I own
I will give to the poor. And Lord, if I have cheated anyone,
I promise to pay them back four times as much as I stole."
9 Jesus said to him, "Your repentance shows that today life has come
to you and your household,
and that you are a true son of Abraham.
10 The Son of Man has come to seek out and to give life to those
who are lost.

2 Corinthians 5:19 NLT

For God was in Christ, reconciling the world to himself, no longer
counting people's sins against them. And he gave us this wonderful
message of reconciliation.

Grace and Peace, Beloved!

Being in the presence of Jesus changes us! It is impossible to encounter Jesus, the Anointed One, and leave the same. The account of Zacchaeus in Luke 19:1-10 is a prime example of this type of change. Let's examine this story more closely.

Zacchaeus made a lot of poor choices in his career. He was stealing money as a tax collector, but Jesus loved him, spent time with him, and forgave him. Zacchaeus changed both his behavior and attitude. He repented. The conversation recorded between Zaccheus and Jesus is limited. We do not see Jesus addressing Zacchaeus' wrongdoing or reprimanding him, although Jesus was fully aware of his sins. What we do see, however, is two things:

1) Jesus telling Zacchaeus that he must stay at Zacchaeus' home, and
2) Zacchaeus testifying of his new attitude and behavior. The new action implies he had experienced an internal change. The presence of Jesus was the change agent.

When we invite Jesus into the home of our hearts, change is inevitable.

Beloved, when I look back on my life, I see many times where I made poor choices. There were times when I purposely walked away from God's way to pursue paths that were selfish and unwise! Frankly, in this past week or so, I can see that I have not always made the best choices. I have asked for forgiveness for all the times I chose to go my own way instead of remaining on God's righteous path for my life. Today, I choose better.

You can also choose better! Soak in the presence of Jesus. Allow his love to wash over you and cooperate with the transformation occurring in your life.

Today's Prayer:

Thank you, Lord, that I am in your presence. I praise you for the transforming power that is working within me. Lord, I want to spend more time with you and allow your goodness to spread throughout my heart. I ask for your wisdom regarding my choices. I yield my will to you. I will no longer make choices without consulting you. Direct me today. In the mighty name of Jesus, I pray! Amen.

I am encouraged! You be encouraged, too!

Day 12

Encounter Him

Psalms 16:11 AMPC

You will show me the path of life; in Your presence is fullness of joy, at Your right hand there are pleasures forevermore.

Exodus 13:21 KJV

And the LORD went before them by day in a pillar of a cloud, to lead them the way; and by night in a pillar of fire, to give them light; to go by day and night:

Psalm 84:1-2 NLT

1 How lovely is your dwelling place, O LORD of Heaven's Armies.
2 I long, yes, I faint with longing to enter the courts of the LORD. With my whole being, body and soul, I will shout joyfully to the living God.

Grace and Peace, Beloved!

As the children of Israel exited Egypt, God's presence was visible. They saw his presence with their natural, physical eyes. There are times

31

when we experience God's glory in a tangible way. Today, let's abide in his presence.

I want to experience the presence of God, Beloved. I want to feel the fullness of joy that is in his presence. I want to feel it, even though I know that we walk by faith and not by our feelings or our natural senses. Hallelujah! Speaking for myself, I wouldn't serve a God I could not feel sometimes.

The Psalmist says that at the Father's right hand are "pleasures forevermore." Desire that pleasure, Beloved, not the fleeting pleasure of this world but the eternal pleasure God has stored up for you. Meditate on all the delightful things he has allocated to you. Know that a joyful believer also knows God's presence!

Today's Prayer:

Lord, may your presence be so heavy on me that even unbelievers will see the supernatural joy upon my life. It is all because of you, Lord! Thank you for the revelation knowledge I receive when reading your word. With that knowledge comes wisdom to relate your word to my life. With wisdom comes action. I will do what you have called me to do. In the mighty name of Jesus, I pray! Amen.

I am encouraged! You be encouraged, too!

Part 3
A New Identity

Day 13

Created Anew

Galatians 2:20 KJV

I am crucified with Christ: nevertheless I live; yet not I, but Christ liveth in me: and the life which I now live in the flesh I live by the faith of the Son of God, who loved me, and gave himself for me.

Ephesians 4:22-24 KJV

22 That ye put off concerning the former conversation the old man, which is corrupt according to the deceitful lusts;
23 And be renewed in the spirit of your mind;
24 And that ye put on the new man, which after God is created in righteousness and true holiness.

2 Corinthians 5:17 KJV

Therefore if any man be in Christ, he is a new creature: old things are passed away; behold, all things are become new.

Grace and Peace, Beloved!

When we accepted the invitation to follow Christ, our spirits were reborn. We became brand new creations in Christ Jesus. Before the Apostle Paul's conversion in Acts 9, he persecuted the church vehemently. Yet, we see him tell the church at Corinth in 2 Corinthians 7 that he and his team have wronged no one. How could he say this with such confidence? It is because Paul understood the dynamics of his conversion. He had been reborn and was no longer his former self. He had been re-created. The old man was dead. (World Changers Church International, 2018).

Jesus loves you and died for you. Your value is so high that Jesus's blood was shed to redeem you. You are an overcomer. No matter what happens on this day, remember you are loved!

Today's Prayer:

Thank you, Father, that nothing can separate me from you. I am no longer my past. You have given me new life, and I am thankful. I exercise my authority over satan, the accuser, and command him to go. In the mighty name of Jesus, I pray! Amen.

I am encouraged! You be encouraged, too!

Day 14

King's Kids

Job 5:9 NLT

He does great things too marvelous to understand.
He performs countless miracles.

Acts 4:29-30 KJV

29 And now, Lord, behold their threatenings: and grant unto thy
servants, that with all boldness they may speak thy word,
30 By stretching forth thine hand to heal; and that signs and wonders
may be done by the name of thy holy child Jesus.

1 Peter 2:9 KJV

But ye are a chosen generation, a royal priesthood, an holy nation, a
peculiar people; that ye should shew forth the praises of him who hath
called you out of darkness into his marvellous light;

Grace and Peace, Beloved!

In order to be believers, we must believe. We are King's kids, Kingdom workers, and Kingdom-minded. We are not of this world so we do not live by the fallacies of the world system. We don't have to believe what the world feeds us. We are here to be and make a difference. We are sanctified and set apart for our Father's glory. Miracles are right there under our noses; we can sense them; we can inhale them.

Separate yourself from the cliques and walk into your royal role, a child of the Most High. Refuse to inhale the lies of satan. Walk according to your spiritual senses not your natural senses. Speak his will and you will have what you say. You have been born again. First, believe in the love of God. God loves you! Do you believe?

Today's Prayer:

Father, I believe. Help my unbelief. Holy Spirit, sharpen my spiritual senses as I yield myself to you. I no longer want to walk this earth as a mere natural man/woman. I know that I am set apart for your glory, and I cooperate with that plan. Thank you for the courage and boldness to proclaim your Word. As I go forth today and in the days to come, miracles, signs, and wonders follow me because I have been granted authority by Jesus Christ. In the mighty name of Jesus, I pray! Amen.

I am encouraged! You be encouraged, too!

Day 15

Whole and Complete

Colossians 2:10 KJV

And ye are complete in him, which is the head of all principality and power:

I Thessalonians 5:23 KJV

And the very God of peace sanctify you wholly; and I pray God your whole spirit and soul and body be preserved blameless unto the coming of our Lord Jesus Christ.

Ephesians 3:19 NLT

And to know the love of Christ, which passeth knowledge, that ye might be filled with all the fulness of God.

Grace and Peace, Beloved!

We are whole and complete in Christ Jesus. His blood purchased us and placed us in right standing with the Father. The Hebrew word, Shalom, conveys that sense of wholeness. We typically think of this word as peace and that is correct. However, it extends beyond that to suggest "a state of fullness and perfection; overflowing inner and outer joy and peaceful serenity (Soroski)."

This wholeness is part of our benefits package when we accept Christ Jesus (Psalm 103:2). Is that not wonderful?

Beloved, remember that the Creator of the universe loves you! You are treasured and priceless. The blood that was shed for you has infinite value. Likewise, your worth is immeasurable. You are whole in Christ, and because of him, you lack no good thing.

Today's Prayer:

Father, I thank you that I am victorious in Christ Jesus. I know that he has fought and won every battle on my behalf. I am bold, strong, and confident – a mighty warrior standing against satan's wiles. I am full of joy, hope, and peace by the power of your Spirit. What a beautiful day to be free! In the mighty name of Jesus, I pray! Amen.

I am encouraged! You be encouraged, too!

Day 16

Esteemed

Psalm 139:14 KJV

I will praise thee; for I am fearfully and wonderfully made: marvellous are thy works; and that my soul knoweth right well.

Matthew 22:37-40 KJV

37 Jesus said unto him, Thou shalt love the Lord thy God with all thy heart, and with all thy soul, and with all thy mind.

38 This is the first and great commandment.

39 And the second is like unto it,

Thou shalt love thy neighbour as thyself.

40 On these two commandments hang all the law and the prophets.

James 3:16 NLT

For wherever there is jealousy and selfish ambition, there you will find disorder and evil of every kind.

Grace and Peace, Beloved!

The love of God within us resolves any feelings of low self-esteem or inadequacy. We are new creations in Christ Jesus with confidence and a healthy view of ourselves. We are made in the image of the Creator. With his love drenching our very souls, we are capable of becoming far more than we could ever dream of on our own! The scriptures tell us to love our neighbors in the same manner that we love ourselves. Clearly, how we love ourselves, encourage ourselves, extend grace to ourselves, and support ourselves plays a critical role in how we love and respond to others. Each one of us is a masterpiece, wonderfully crafted by the Master. Jealousy, strife, competition, and other selfish attitudes have no place in Christ. Each of us is secure in our identity as a son or daughter of the Most High God.

As you meditate today, ask the Holy Spirit to help you with any unhealthy views of yourself. He is here to help. Remember that you are loved unconditionally.

Today's Prayer:

Father, help me to understand that my identity is in you. True security in who I am is connected to my value as your creation. Thank you for making me so fearfully, fiercely, and wonderfully. I love myself with your love. I see myself as you see me, through the lens of the blood of Jesus Christ. In the mighty name of Jesus, I pray! Amen.

I am encouraged! You be encouraged, too!

Day 17

No More Shame

Romans 8:1 KJV

There is therefore now no condemnation to them which are in Christ Jesus, who walk not after the flesh, but after the Spirit.

Galatians 5:1, 16 KJV

1 Stand fast therefore in the liberty wherewith Christ hath made us free, and be not entangled again with the yoke of bondage. 16 This I say then, Walk in the Spirit, and ye shall not fulfil the lust of the flesh.

Proverbs 20:27 KJV

The spirit of man is the candle of the Lord, searching all the inward parts of the belly.

Psalm 34:4-5 KJV

4 I sought the LORD, and he heard me,
and delivered me from all my fears.
5 They looked unto him, and were lightened:
and their faces were not ashamed.

Colossians 1:13 KJV

Who hath delivered us from the power of darkness,

and hath translated us into the kingdom of his dear Son:

Grace and Peace, Beloved!

The Helper is here to help. He helps us detach from shame, guilt, and condemnation. As we walk with him, we walk in the light. It is amazing that our Father not only instructs us, but he gives us the support, the Holy Spirit, to help us follow the instructions. We are so loved! We are in Christ.

Stay focused on walking in the Spirit, Beloved. With that focus, worldly concerns and lust will disappear and have no power over you. Walk with your head held high embracing the magnitude of what Christ has done.

Today's Prayer:

Father, I ask that you help me walk in the Spirit so that I do not fulfill the works of the flesh. Holy Spirit, I want to be led by you. I submit myself to your leading. I come against sin cycles which try to enslave me. I rebuke every plan of the enemy designed to interrupt my day, and I release your peace.

I walk in this world as your chosen one, a world changer, and an atmosphere shifter. I overcome by the blood of the Lamb and the word of my testimony.

By faith, I thank you in advance for what you are doing in the lives of my family members and in my relationships with loved ones and friends. I thank you, Lord, for what you have already done in my life. I walk in victory and make spiritual progress. In the mighty name of Jesus, I pray. Amen!

I am encouraged! You be encouraged, too!

Day 18

Walk in Confidence

Psalm 118:6 KJV

The LORD is on my side; I will not fear: what can man do unto me?

Proverbs 3:26 KJV

For the LORD shall be thy confidence, and shall keep thy foot from being taken.

1 John 3:20-21 KJV

20 For if our heart condemn us, God is greater than our heart, and knoweth all things.
21 Beloved, if our heart condemn us not, then have we confidence toward God.

Grace and Peace, Beloved!

The blessings of the Lord are many. We must stay humble and position ourselves to receive. His grace is sufficient for all that we need. Knowing the enormity of his grace and provision helps us to obey without delay. At times, we all stalled to act upon God's directives; this procrastination or disobedience can lead to thoughts of condemnation. Again, his grace is sufficient. Like David, we can quickly repent (change our minds and go a different way) and submit to the word of God. We have confidence that the Father's love far surpasses any accusation, and we are in right standing with him. Believing God's Word, yielding to it, and agreeing with it is the highest form of submission and obedience.

Whatever you do, Beloved, do not live in denial of the Father's precious promises! Live in confidence knowing that God is for you and is more than this world against you. Follow his heart.

Today's Prayer:

Father, I thank you for your love. Your love is all encompassing. I thank you for blessing me richly. Your riches are inexhaustible. Help me to understand more clearly your plan for my life. As I ask according to your will, I have the things I have ask for. I trust and believe you. In the mighty name of Jesus, I pray! Amen.

I am encouraged! You Be encouraged, too!!

Day 19

A New Mind

Romans 12:2 KJV

And be not conformed to this world: but be ye transformed by the renewing of your mind, that ye may prove what is that good, and acceptable, and perfect, will of God.

Matthew 16:19 KJV

And I will give unto thee the keys of the kingdom of heaven: and whatsoever thou shalt bind on earth shall be bound in heaven: and whatsoever thou shalt loose on earth shall be loosed in heaven.

John 17:16 KJV

They are not of the world, even as I am not of the world.

Grace and Peace, Beloved!

How do we make our minds new again? First of all, we must recognize that we are not of this world. We are of the Kingdom of God. The renewing of the mind goes against world systems, ideologies, ways of being, and ways of doing. Therefore, we walk and flow in the supernatural. Secondly, we are to pour the word of God into our minds so that we can think exactly like God. God's mind is also the mind of Jesus which is also the mind of the Holy Spirit. Jesus came to do the will of the Father; and the Holy Spirit only speaks what the Father says. Their minds are one. We pray and speak the Father's will to be done. We delve into the word to learn what that will is. We bring heaven to earth. We do not allow anything contrary to heavenly order to operate in our lives. Thirdly, we rely on the power of the Holy Spirit to point us to thinking like Christ! The culture of this world may say, "Everyone has to die of something" while a renewed mind speaks on this wise, "The Father satisfies me with long life and shows me His salvation (Psalm 91:16 KJV - paraphrased)."

Now, go be transformed (you got this because the Holy Spirit helps you) by the renewing of your mind.

Today's Prayer:

Father, I thank you for giving me the tools to renew my mind. I am a new creation in you; old things are passed away. The Holy Spirit helps me with everything. As I spend time with you and read your word today, I receive revelation knowledge and wisdom to operate as a child of the King, bringing heaven into the earth realm. My mind thinks differently and I am walking in the supernatural. In the mighty name of Jesus, I pray! Amen.

I am encouraged! You be encouraged, too!

Day 20

Ongoing Fellowship

Mark 1:35 KJV

And in the morning, rising up a great while before day, he went out, and departed into a solitary place, and there prayed.

Psalm 143:6 KJV

I stretch forth my hands unto thee: my soul thirsteth after thee, as a thirsty land. Selah.

Luke 11:3 KJV

Give us day by day our daily bread.

Jeremiah 29:11 KJV

For I know the thoughts that I think toward you, saith the Lord, thoughts of peace, and not of evil, to give you an expected end.

Grace and Peace, Beloved!

How wonderful it is to be in Christ! We have a new way of thinking, believing, and carrying ourselves in this earth. Building on the previous devotional on renewing our minds, let's realize that the renewal process is ongoing. The world constantly bombards us with its ways, most of which misaligns with God's ways. To combat those outside influences, we develop daily fellowship with God in our own way. Ongoing fellowship with the Father is paramount to a Godly life.

On a personal note, some days I don't even notice my own needs. Yet, other days, I am heavy with the weight of them. My response is to seek the Lord wholeheartedly. I know that when I look for him, I always find him. In fact, he is living in me. I can connect with him through my spirit and receive the answers that I need.

Develop your own schedule or pattern of communicating with the Father. Your relationship with him is critical to receiving direction on his master plan for your life.

Today's Prayer:

Thank you, Father, for being here for me. I need you every moment of my life. I will find a quiet place today, away from this busy world, and listen for your voice. Speak to me, dear Lord. I want my communication with you to become my norm until God's manifested glory becomes my reality - until my thoughts and way of life become one with your word. In the mighty name of Jesus, I pray! Amen.

I am encouraged! You be encouraged, too!

Day 21

God's Breath

Genesis 2:7 KJV

And the LORD God formed man of the dust of the ground, and breathed into his nostrils the breath of life; and man became a living soul.

Acts 17:28 KJV

For in him we live, and move, and have our being; as certain also of your own poets have said, For we are also his offspring.

Psalm 91:16 KJV

With long life will I satisfy him, and shew him my salvation.

1 John 4:18 KJV

There is no fear in love; but perfect love casteth out fear: because fear hath torment. He that feareth is not made perfect in love.

Grace and Peace, Beloved!

Our very breath is a gift from God. Through God's action, man became a living soul. We are literally living out the breath of God every day. That concept is so monumental. Let's steward God's breath faithfully and handle his breath with care.

Before you pray the prayer below, complete this breathing exercise. Take three deep breaths, inhaling and exhaling slowly. Be very conscious of your breathing. Follow the exercise with the prayer taking time to really embrace every word.

Today's Prayer:

Father, as I inhale today, I cover myself with the benefits of salvation. As I breathe in, every cell of my body responds to your promise of long life. I breathe in your grace.

I breathe out any worries that try to attach themselves to me; I expel care and cast it upon Christ Jesus.

I breathe in the peace and power of the Holy Spirit. My being is filled with boldness and courage.

I exhale any fear because I live in God's perfect love.
I thank you, Father, that you alone fill me up. All is well with me. In the mighty name of Jesus, I pray! Amen.

I am encouraged! You be encouraged, too!

Part 4
Benefits of
Salvation

Day 22

Freedom and Forgiveness of Sin

Galatians 5:1, 13 NLT

1 So Christ has truly set us free. Now make sure that you stay free, and don't get tied up again in slavery to the law.
13 For you have been called to live in freedom, my brothers and sisters. But don't use your freedom to satisfy your sinful nature. Instead, use your freedom to serve one another in love.

1 Peter 2:24 NLT

He personally carried our sins in his body on the cross so that we can be dead to sin and live for what is right.
By his wounds you are healed.

Hebrews 10:10 TPT

By God's will we have been purified and made holy once and for all through the sacrifice of the body of Jesus, the Messiah!

Grace and Peace, Beloved!

When we repented and turned to Jesus Christ, all of our sin - past, present, and future - was forgiven. Now we are free and at liberty to live a holy life. Christ has already sanctified us, set us apart, for Kingdom work. After we come to Christ, any missteps we make are already under the blood of Jesus. Christ purified us once and for all. His work is finished.

In my own life, occasionally I can lose sight of the victory I have in Christ. The Holy Spirit reminds me that I am forgiven and that Jesus has already prayed for me.

Jesus has already prayed for you too, Beloved. Remember his words regarding having prayed for you.

John 17:15-17, 20 NIV
15 My prayer is not that you take them out of the world
but that you protect them from the evil one.
16 They are not of the world, even as I am not of it.
17 Sanctify them by the truth; your word is truth.
20 My prayer is not for them alone. I pray also for those who will
believe in me through their message,

There may be times when you feel like you are surrounded by evil on all sides and in the midst of deep waters. Jesus has prayed that you are protected from the evil one. Be confident that his prayers never fail.

Today's Prayer:

Father, thank you for forgiving me once and for all. The blood of Jesus has cleansed me of all unrighteousness. I do not intentionally gravitate towards my old ways, but even when I do, I am still yours. I am yours forever. I look into the mirror of the word and make the necessary adjustments to align with your will. I turn quickly and resume my righteous path. In the mighty name of Jesus, I pray! Amen.

I am encouraged! You be encouraged, too!

Day 23

All of God's Goodness

Lamentations 3:22-23 KJV

22 It is of the LORD's mercies that we are not consumed, because his compassions fail not.

23 They are new every morning: great is thy faithfulness.

Acts 17:24, 26 KJV

24 God that made the world and all things therein, seeing that he is Lord of heaven and earth, dwelleth not in temples made with hands;

26 And hath made of one blood all nations of men for to dwell on all the face of the earth, and hath determined the times before appointed, and the bounds of their habitation;

Ephesians 1:4 KJV

According as he hath chosen us in him before the foundation of the world, that we should be holy and without blame before him in love:

Grace and Peace, Beloved!

How glorious it is that we are here, in this new day, to experience all of God's goodness. Before he formed the world, the Father predestined us to be alive in this hour to share in his glory! We are here at this appointed time to receive and dispense his love. Let us be about our Father's business.

I am so excited about God's magnificent plan for my life. I pray that you are, too! Know that God's perfect plan for your life far exceeds all you could ever ask, imagine, or think. Pray in heaven's language and believe that the Holy Spirit will reveal to you every step that you must take today. As he directs, possess your land. Go forth and be great!

Today's Prayer:

Father, I am overjoyed to be in your presence and to be your child. Your love washes over me and dispels all of my fears. My focus today and every day is to please you in words and in deeds. Help me to walk out this marvelous life and to bring honor to your name. I want my walk to match my talk. As I meditate on things eternal, my desire is to hear you say, "Well done!" In the mighty name of Jesus, I pray! Amen.

I am encouraged! You be encouraged, too!

Day 24

He Satisfies

Psalm 19:9-10 KJV

9 The fear of the LORD is clean, enduring for ever:
the judgments of the LORD are true and righteous altogether.
10 More to be desired are they than gold, yea, than much fine gold:
sweeter also than honey and the honeycomb.

Psalm 34:8 KJV

O taste and see that the LORD is good: blessed is the man that trusteth
in him.

Psalm 103:5 KJV

Who satisfieth thy mouth with good things; so that thy youth is
renewed like the eagle's.

Grace and Peace, Beloved!

The Lord is sweeter than the honey in the honeycomb! Life with him becomes sweeter each day. My oh my, is that not the ultimate life? He completely satisfies us with good things. He fulfills all we could ever need for this day. We need not worry about tomorrow. We have mercy, compassion, grace, kindness, and love for today. We are confident in knowing we can come to him daily for all that is needed.

I love Jesus so much; he loves me more. Oh, what a matchless love! I thank him that he is positioning me to be exactly where I need to be. I am in perfect rhythm with him.

Trust him, today, to fill you to overflowing with the good and abundant life.

Today's Prayer:

Thank you, Father, that you shape my desires to mirror what you desire for my life. I desire more of you; there is life-joy in wanting more of you. Pure life satisfaction is in you. I am excited about how you will make my wildest dreams come true. Give me eyes to see you, Father, in everything. In the mighty name of Jesus, I pray! Amen.

I am encouraged! You be encouraged, too!

Day 25

Protection

Isaiah 54:17 KJV

*No weapon that is formed against thee shall prosper; and every tongue that shall rise against thee in judgment thou shalt condemn. This is the heritage of the servants of the L*ORD*, and their righteousness is of me, saith the L*ORD*.*

2 Thessalonians 3:3 NIV

But the Lord is faithful, and he will strengthen you and protect you from the evil one.

Psalm 138:7 NIV

Though I walk in the midst of trouble, you preserve my life. You stretch out your hand against the anger of my foes; with your right hand you save me.

Grace and Peace, Beloved!

God is good all the time. He will continually protect you; He will never leave you nor forsake you. His presence is always with you for the Spirit of God is on the inside of you. He shelters you during life's difficulties. Wherever you are, he is.

Today's Prayer:

I am praying these words over you today. Agree with this prayer.

Beloved, may his love overwhelm you! May his power protect you. May you be guarded by his presence. May his light surround you. I plead the blood of Jesus over you and each of your family members. No weapon or scheme of the enemy will ever prevail against you. You are protected from sickness and disease. Regardless of what your circumstance is saying, your assurance is in Jesus Christ. Your hope is in the Lord! In the mighty name of Jesus, I pray! Amen.

I am encouraged! You be encouraged, too!

Day 26

Deliverance

Psalm 34:17, 19 KJV

*17 The righteous cry, and the Lord heareth, and delivereth
them out of all their troubles.
19 Many are the afflictions of the righteous: but the Lord
delivereth him out of them all.*

Daniel 3:17 KJV

*If it be so, our God whom we serve is able to deliver us from the
burning fiery furnace,
and he will deliver us out of thine hand, O king.*

Psalm 18:2 KJV

*The LORD is my rock, and my fortress, and my deliverer; my God, my
strength, in whom I will trust;
my buckler, and the horn of my salvation, and my high tower.*

Grace and Peace, Beloved!

We believe our God! His word is true. He delivers us from every trouble; not one trouble is left out. Salvation and deliverance are inseparable. They go hand in hand. The very meaning of salvation encompasses deliverance.

According to Merriam-Webster's dictionary, key definitions of *salvation* are as follows (Merriam-Webster, n.d.):

1) deliverance from the power and effects of sin,
2) preservation from destruction or failure, and
3) deliverance from danger or difficulty

When we receive Christ, deliverance is immediately accessible. Deliverance is a promise.

Receive your deliverance today. You may be facing a multitude of challenges but trust in the only Living God. Rest in the promise. By grace through faith, you are the righteousness of God! Now that should put a smile on your face and a pep in your spirit.

Today's Prayer:

Thank you, Father, that I am delivered from all troubles. I receive my deliverance now by faith. Holy Spirit, thank you for helping me. Thank you for causing me to remember who I am in Christ. I walk confidently in what Christ has done for me. I am healed, rescued, saved, preserved, liberated, and delivered. I agree with the word of God concerning my status, my right standing with you. I speak the word over myself. In the mighty name of Jesus, I pray! Amen.

I am encouraged! You be encouraged, too!

Day 27

Refuge and Safety

Psalm 9:9 KJV

The LORD also will be a refuge for the oppressed, a refuge in times of trouble.

Psalm 146:9 KJV

The LORD preserveth the strangers; he relieveth the fatherless and widow: but the way of the wicked he turneth upside down.

Psalm 62:8 KJV

Trust in him at all times; ye people, pour out your heart before him: God is a refuge for us. Selah.

Grace and Peace, Beloved!

It is hard to write about "refuge" without imagining the plight of refugees, those persons fleeing violence or harm from their own countries to find safety in another. The refugee's goal is to locate protection, security, and help. If we can think, for a moment, about the that level of desperation in order to find rest, we can grasp more clearly the significance of "refuge." God encompasses that level of rest (safety, protection, security, and help). Let's run to him.

Believe God, Beloved, to be that safe place for you. Trust him. He will protect your heart.

Today's Prayer:

Father, I make room for you today. I make room for you in my home, which is my physical safe place. I allow my home to be your sanctuary, a place where your peace is present for me and all who enter. I make room for you in my life because I am not my own. I belong to you. Indeed you are the Lord of my life. I pray for those who have no sense of safety that you would bring them supernatural resources to stabilize their lives. Help them to truly know you as the place of refuge. Give them rest. Have your way in me today. In the mighty name of Jesus, I pray! Amen.

I am encouraged! You be encouraged, too!

Day 28

Household Well-Being

Acts 16:30-32 KJV

30 And brought them out, and said, Sirs, what must I do to be saved?
31 And they said, Believe on the Lord Jesus Christ, and thou shalt be saved, and thy house.
32 And they spake unto him the word of the Lord, and to all that were in his house.

Acts 11:13-14 KJV

13 And he shewed us how he had seen an angel in his house, which stood and said unto him, Send men to Joppa, and call for Simon, whose surname is Peter;
14 Who shall tell thee words, whereby thou and all thy house shall be saved.

Genesis 7:1 KJV

And the Lord said unto Noah, Come thou and all thy house into the ark; for thee have I seen righteous before me in this generation.

Psalm 133:1 KJV

Behold, how good and how pleasant it is for brethren to dwell together in unity!

Psalm 112:1-3 NIV

1 Praise the Lord. Blessed are those who fear the Lord, who find great delight in his commands.

2 Their children will be mighty in the land; the generation of the upright will be blessed.

3 Wealth and riches are in their houses, and their righteousness endures forever.

Grace and Peace, Beloved!

The Father cares about all about which we care. We care about our families and so does he. The scriptures listed above show how one believing person can lead to salvation for the entire household. Our households or family members receive the overflow of goodness that has been imparted to our lives. That overflowing cup of goodness spills over to bless them.

Continue to pray for your household. Pray and believe that each family member will respond to the love of God and accept Jesus as Lord and Savior. Pray for the well-being of each family member and for your family as a whole. Declare that your household leaves a legacy of righteousness, wealth, and riches.

Today's Prayer:

Father, thank you that my household and family members are eager to serve you. I plead and apply the blood of Jesus over each one of them. Our family is whole, unified, and at peace. All of our material needs are met. There is not one feeble member among us. My household leaves a legacy of righteousness, wealth, and riches. In the mighty name of Jesus, I pray! Amen.

I am encouraged! You be encouraged, too!

Day 29

Recovery

I Samuel 30:8 KJV

And David enquired at the Lord, saying, Shall I pursue after this troop? shall I overtake them?

And he answered him, Pursue: for thou shalt surely overtake them, and without fail recover all.

Romans 12:19 KJV

Dearly beloved, avenge not yourselves, but rather give place unto wrath: for it is written,

Vengeance is mine; I will repay, saith the Lord.

Isaiah 35:4 KJV

Say to them that are of a fearful heart, Be strong, fear not: behold, your God will come with vengeance,

even God with a recompence; he will come and save you.

Grace and Peace, Beloved!

The Father is our personal God! Let that sit for a moment. It is hard to conceptualize how our Father knows each one of us by name. Yet, he knows us intimately and has a one-on-one relationship with each one of us. The Father knew each one of us before he carefully crafted us in the womb. He knew each of us before the world was formed. He sees us right now, in this very moment, and all that we are experiencing. The Holy Spirit speaks to us personally. We don't need a third person to speak to us; Jesus Christ is our High Priest and we can go straight to the throne of grace to obtain the grace and mercy that we need.

With that established, know that if you have suffered loss in any capacity, our Father is the God of Recompense. We can trust Him to right wrongs, rectify injustices, repay evil, and restore losses. Thank him for being the One who ensures that we recover all!

Today's Prayer:

Father, thank you for awaking me this morning to a new, delightful day. I believe that I am happy, healthy, whole, and healed because of your Grace. Thank you that I am able to live out your breath and purpose for me on this day. You are my healer, my miracle worker, and my strong deliverer. I totally depend on you for recovery, recompense, retribution, and restoration of every thing that the enemy has stolen. Holy Spirit, I know that you have gone ahead of me to make every crooked place straight. You are opening doors that no man can shut and closing doors that no man can open. Your divine leading keeps me on your righteous path.

Speak to my heart and give me opportunities today to point others (believers who need to believe again as well as non-believers) to you! Thank you for your everlasting love. In the mighty name of Jesus, I pray. Amen!

I am encouraged! You be encouraged, too!

Day 30

Physical Healing and Health

3 John 1:2 KJV

Beloved, I wish above all things that thou mayest prosper and be in health, even as thy soul prospereth.

Psalm 103:2-3 KJV

2 Bless the LORD, O my soul, and forget not all his benefits:
3 Who forgiveth all thine iniquities; who healeth all thy diseases;

Grace and Peace, Beloved!

The Father's good plan for us is wholeness in every area. This plan includes healing and divine health. The name of Jesus is above every name; his name is higher than any disease, sickness, or illness that can be recorded in the most complex medical journal. The Father wants us to be healthy, happy, prosperous, pain free, without stress, and successful. Take your healing today!

Today's Prayer:

Father, I decree and declare to my body that I am healthy and physically fit. Sickness and disease are far from me. By the stripes of Jesus, I am healed. He has already paid the price. I praise you, Father, that I am pain free and without stress. Every cell of my body conforms to the healing virtue of Jesus.

I praise you now, Father, and I rest in the finished work of Jesus Christ. In the mighty name of Jesus, I pray. Amen!

I am encouraged! You be encouraged, too!

Day 31

All Healing

Isaiah 10:27 KJV

And it shall come to pass in that day, that his burden shall be taken away from off thy shoulder, and his yoke from off thy neck, and the yoke shall be destroyed because of the anointing.

Isaiah 53:5 KJV

But he was wounded for our transgressions, he was bruised for our iniquities: the chastisement of our peace was upon him; and with his stripes we are healed.

Psalm 34:17 KJV

The righteous cry, and the LORD heareth, and delivereth them out of all their troubles.

Grace and Peace, Beloved!

The scriptures tell us that the anointing destroys every yoke in our lives. We receive that. Because of the yoke-destroying, bondage-breaking power of Jesus Christ, our souls and our bodies now function according to divine order and protocol. We tell our spirit man to take ascendancy and be led by the Holy Spirit. We are Spirit-filled. We decree that we are healed on every level.

I agree with you today, Beloved.

Today's Prayer:

Father, I thank you that I am healed emotionally, physically, psychologically, spiritually, and financially because it is the will of God that I be. I pray his will!

I will keep a praise on my lips today and the Holy Spirit is here to remind me of the Father's promises. When trouble arises, I continue to give thanks knowing trouble does not last; it is only temporal. Thank you, Father, for perfecting all that concerns me. You are my constant. You are always with me. Always! May the words of my mouth and the meditations of my heart be acceptable to you. Glory be to God! In the mighty name of Jesus, I pray! Amen.

I am encouraged! You be encouraged, too!

Part 5
Soul Healing

Day 32

Healing for Our Souls

Psalm 147:3-4 KJV

He healeth the broken in heart, and bindeth up their wounds.

Isaiah 61:1 KJV

The Spirit of the Lord God is upon me; because the Lord hath anointed me to preach good tidings unto the meek; he hath sent me to bind up the brokenhearted, to proclaim liberty to the captives, and the opening of the prison to them that are bound;

Grace and Peace,Beloved!

Christ has come to heal broken hearts. We may have soul wounds so deeply buried within our hearts that they are difficult to articulate. Perhaps we cannot understand why we find ourselves repeating the same self-sabotaging behaviors over and over again. Maybe, like a magnet, we constantly draw people into our lives who bring us harm. It is time to be healed in our souls (our minds, will, intellect, emotions, and even our personalities). The Father desires us to be whole and at peace with nothing missing or broken in our lives. He knows all. Jesus Christ paid the price to perfect ALL that concerns us including both our conscious and unconscious flaws. It is already done. We simply cooperate with the finished work!

Today's Prayer:

Holy Spirit, I thank you for revealing to me any broken places in my soul that need healing. I yield my soul to you and submit to the healing process. I know that you go before me and level every obstacle that would try to impede my progress. Father, thank you for delivering me from the oppression of emotional blackmail, emotional attachments, demonic soul ties, malicious gossip, toxic relationships, and all variations of these soul vandals. My mind is renewed to your word only. I rest in the finished work of Jesus Christ and know that his work is full and complete, never half-done. I am saved, redeemed, delivered, secure, safe, and set free! In the mighty name of Jesus, I pray. Amen!

I am encouraged! You be encouraged, too!

Day 33

Help! I Am Disappointed in God!

Psalms 27:14 TPT

Here's what I've learned through it all: Don't give up; don't be impatient;
be entwined as one with the Lord. Be brave and courageous, and
never lose hope.
Yes, keep on waiting—for he will never disappoint you!

Isaiah 55:8-9 KJV

8 For my thoughts are not your thoughts, neither are your ways my
ways, saith the LORD.
9 For as the heavens are higher than the earth, so are my ways higher
than your ways, and my thoughts than your thoughts.

Proverbs 3:5 MSG

Trust God from the bottom of your heart;
don't try to figure out everything on your own.

Grace and Peace, Beloved!

The Father cares about our emotional well-being. Yes, even our disappointments. Don't be disappointed when you think God did not do what you expected. If we feel disappointed in God, let's just establish that the enemy is lying again because our Father never disappoints.

I speak from personal experience because I have been there, too! Know that God gives me nothing to share with you unless it applies to me first! I am being very transparent. Lingering disappointment can be a sign of pride and arrogance, Beloved. Let's submit ourselves to God and remain in the "submissive" mode. Even when things do not turn out the way that we planned, God has a perfect plan – more perfect than any plan we could create. Put your trust in him again, without wavering, doubting, or pouting! God will never forget about you. You are his, and he desires to bring you to full maturity.

Today's Prayer:

Father, thank you for caring for me even when I feel disappointed. I am your child and you desire to bring me to full spiritual maturity. As I develop, I am moving to another level in you – no longer a babe who drinks milk but an adult who eats meat. I submit to your "mission" even when you say "no." You never leave me, never forsake me, and never ignore me. My valley experiences are merely places where I learn to trust you more. I use those places, those events, and those times to draw closer to you. I bless you at all times! In the mighty name of Jesus, I pray! Amen.

I am encouraged! You be encouraged, too!

Day 34

Help! I Am Disappointed in Others!

Isaiah 41:10 KJV

Fear thou not; for I am with thee: be not dismayed; for I am thy God:
I will strengthen thee;
yea, I will help thee; yea, I will uphold thee with the right hand of my
righteousness.

Psalm 118:6 KJV

The LORD is on my side; I will not fear: what can man do unto me?

Romans 5:5 AMPC

Such hope never disappoints or deludes or shames us, for God's love
has been poured out in our hearts
through the Holy Spirit Who has been given to us.

Grace and Peace, Beloved!

Disappointment is a part of life. How we handle disappointment and what we do with it is a critical part of our healing. Even when others do not live up to our expectations, we can rest in knowing that God never

84

disappoints. We can roll that disappointment, that emotional stress, onto Jesus as he envelops us in his precious love and care.

Have you been disappointed or hurt by someone you love? Trust in the one who is dependable. God will ALWAYS be there for you. Choose to believe he is all you need. He promised never to leave you nor forsake you! You can tell him everything. He is completely trustworthy. Below is an additional promise, Beloved, for you to hold close to your heart with passion! Continue to pray. He hears you every time you pray. I am agreeing with you in prayer as well.

Psalms 18:30-31 NLT

30 God's way is perfect. All the Lord's promises prove true.
He is a shield for all who look to Him for protection.
31 For who is God except the Lord? Who but our God is a solid
rock?

Today's Prayer:

Father, when I am disappointed, I know you are there for me. I give this emotional pain to Jesus. Help me to not hold others to such a high standard that they are unable to meet my expectations. Likewise, I realize there are times when I have disappointed others, sometimes knowingly. Your love covers all. I demonstrate your love in my relationships with others. I extend grace, and I receive grace. Thank you, Father, for being all that I need. In the mighty name of Jesus, I pray! Amen.

I am encouraged! You be encouraged, too!

Day 35

Overcoming Depression

Proverbs 18:21 KJV

Death and life are in the power of the tongue: and they that love it shall eat the fruit thereof.

Psalm 42:5 KJV

Why art thou cast down, O my soul? and why art thou disquieted in me? hope thou in God:
for I shall yet praise him for the help of his countenance.

Psalm 30:11 KJV

Thou hast turned for me my mourning into dancing: thou hast put off my sackcloth, and girded me with gladness;

Grace and Peace, Beloved!

My heart is heavy today for those experiencing depression. Are you depressed? Reflect on what you are telling yourself and the narratives you are playing over in your mind. How we talk to ourselves is so important. Meditating on or rehearsing the problem does three things:

1) strengthens the situation,

2) charges our atmosphere with negativity, and

3) becomes a sort of self-fulfilling prophecy that continues our depression.

Fear not, Beloved. You have the solution. The Holy Spirit is here to comfort you in all situations. Ask him to remind you of his word. Make him your priority. Before getting on the phone to talk with your best friend, talk with him. He is a gentleman and is waiting for you to ask for help. He will remind you of his word, his grace, his mercy, and his love.

Today's Prayer:

Father, I thank you for delivering me from depression. You have strengthened me with your might to be able to reject negative thoughts. I resist the attack of the enemy in my thought life. I reject those thoughts that go against the knowledge of Christ. I know Christ and how he has delivered me. Jesus Christ is more real than depression; spirit of depression, I command you to bow to the name of Jesus. My soul is healed; the effects of toxic thoughts and ungodly soul ties is reversed. Healing is my bread. In the mighty name of Jesus I pray. Amen!

I am encouraged! You be encouraged, too!

Day 36

Overcoming Loneliness

Psalm 27:10 VOICE

Even if my father and mother abandon me, the Lord will hold me close.

John 14:16 KJV

And I will pray the Father, and he shall give you another Comforter, that he may abide with you for ever;

John 10:10 KJV

The thief cometh not, but for to steal, and to kill, and to destroy: I am come that they might have life, and that they might have it more abundantly.

Grace and Peace, Beloved!

Today, my heart is for those who are feeling lonely. The word of God is the answer. There is life, love, and peace in the word of God! The Father talks to us through the word. Jesus draws near to us through the word. The Holy Spirit comforts us through the word. Life has exciting things in store for us, and we refuse to settle for where we are now. God is preparing us for our destiny. He prunes our branches along the way in order for us to produce much fruit! We are destined for abundant life!

When you are lonely and feeling down, read God's word! In fact, read the word aloud to speak into your own spirit. Allow your vision to be larger than anything in your past or present. Embrace your big, bright future in Jesus Christ. I hope you are living life everyday expecting God to do great things in your life. May you receive a sudden blessing!

Today's Prayer:

Father of Peace, I thank you for your love. I come boldly to your throne to receive your grace and mercy. I am grateful. Thank you for supernatural rest as I trust in you. You know me by name; you are my friend. I thank you, Lord, for the wisdom and knowledge I receive today from your word and from my intimate time with you. Your word is alive in me. In the mighty name of Jesus, I pray! Amen.

I am encouraged! You be encouraged, too!

Day 37

Overcoming Discontentment and Dissatisfaction

Philippians 4:11-13 KJV

11 Not that I speak in respect of want: for I have learned, in whatsoever state I am, therewith to be content.

12 I know both how to be abased, and I know how to abound: every where and in all things I am instructed both to be full and to be hungry, both to abound and to suffer need.

13 I can do all things through Christ which strengtheneth me.

2 Corinthians 10:12 VOICE

For we would never dare to compare ourselves with people who have based their worth on self-commendation. They check themselves against and compare themselves with one another. It just shows that they don't have any sense!

Isaiah 55:2 VOICE

I don't understand why you spend your money for things that don't nourish or work so hard for what leaves you empty. Attend to Me and eat what is good; enjoy the richest, most delectable of things.

Revelation 1:8 KJV

I am Alpha and Omega, the beginning and the ending, saith the Lord, which is, and which was, and which is to come, the Almighty.

Grace and Peace, Beloved!

In Philippians 4, the Apostle Paul shares his ability to be content in all circumstances. Sometimes we allow discontentment in our hearts by focusing on the wrong things. For example, we may permit our present struggles to overshadow our past blessings and history with the Father. Other times, it is just the opposite. We may feel dissatisfied because we are stuck in the past, forgetting the blessings of today! Yet, other times we may compare ourselves to others and feel that we don't measure up. In these instances, we need to shift our focus.

Renew your joy today, Beloved! The Father has always been with you and always will be. Think on and write down the good you find in every situation. Let thankfulness arise.

Today's Prayer:

Father, help me to be content in every situation. I trust you to direct my path. You chose me before the foundation of the world and are satisfied with me. My focus is sharp and fixed on you. I measure up to your standard; I am in perfect standing with you. In the mighty name of Jesus, I pray! Amen.

I am encouraged! You be encouraged, too!

Day 38

Working Through Discouragement

Galatians 6:9 AMP

Let us not grow weary or become discouraged in doing good, for at the proper time we will reap, if we do not give in

Psalm 7:9 AMPC

Oh, let the wickedness of the wicked come to an end, but establish the [uncompromisingly] righteous [those upright and in harmony with You]; for You, Who try the hearts and emotions and thinking powers, are a righteous God.

Deuteronomy 31:8 NIV

The LORD himself goes before you and will be with you; he will never leave you nor forsake you. Do not be afraid; do not be discouraged.

Grace and Peace, Beloved!

The Father's love is so expansive that it covers every soft place within our hearts. Jesus has already handled our grief as we read in Isaiah 53:4 (KJV).

> *Surely he hath borne our griefs, and carried our sorrows: yet we did esteem him stricken, smitten of God, and afflicted.*

He has provided the remedy for our emotional pain.

Yes, I get discouraged sometimes when I do not see significant change in my life. Beloved, I get impatient but then realize that change is a process; it does not come overnight. In those times, I ask the Lord to stimulate my faith, increase my patience, and give me a new way of thinking. Lasting transformation takes a life time as we move from glory to glory. We are walking on this faith journey for the rest of our days.

When the Father called you, he foresaw the times that you would experience discouragement. In his far-reaching love plan for you, he provided the solution. Know that he is with you in the valley; he is still leading and guiding you. He never leaves you to wander hopelessly all by yourself. Cast aside fear and discouragement today, Beloved! You have the authority to do that because of Jesus Christ.

Today's Prayer:

Father, I thank you for your boundless love for me. I know for sure that your love never fails. I belong to you! I am your work in progress; I trust you to work in me at just the right pace! I totally depend on you for you have promised to complete the good work you started in me. In the mighty name of Jesus, I pray! Amen.

I am encouraged! You be encouraged, too!

Day 39

Recognizing Triggers

Jeremiah 17:14 KJV
Heal me, O LORD, and I shall be healed;
save me, and I shall be saved, for you are my praise.

James 5:16 KJV
Confess your faults one to another, and pray one for another, that ye
may be healed.
The effectual fervent prayer of a righteous man availeth much.

Grace and Peace, Beloved!

Unhealed trauma can leave a brokenness in our souls. We may have areas in our subconscious that remain unhealed because we are not even consciously aware of the deep wounds of trauma. We may feel that we are fine until some incident or confrontation triggers a flood of negative feelings, brokenness, memories, or emotional instability. We may have developed spiritually as much as we know how to the extent of our present understanding. It is time for more.

Allow the Holy Spirit to reveal any infirmity in your soul. He will show you the places that need healing and correct you. Go deeper and accept the healing. Yield to the healing process. If that means therapy, yield to it. If that means sharing your pain with an accountability partner whom you trust, yield to that avenue. Ask the Holy Spirit to reveal to you the person(s) who will protect your heart.

My testimony is this: I was unable to see those fractured places in my soul because I had never allowed myself to genuinely open all the places that appeared to be right on the surface. It is hard to change what we cannot see to change. Opening up those places leads to acknowledgment and puts us on that righteous path of healing.

Today's Prayer:

Thank you, Father, for your divine healing in my soul. I declare that as I sleep, healing of my heart takes place. Your peace washes over me as I sleep. Holy Spirit, show me your righteous path, correct me, and teach me. Reveal your truth to me. I want to be made whole! Thank you for your insight about me, (Insert Your Name Here)! I yield to the healing. In the mighty name of Jesus, I pray! Amen.

I am encouraged! You be encouraged, too!

Day 40

I Am Never Alone

John 14:16 KJV

And I will pray the Father, and he shall give you another Comforter,
that he may abide with you for ever;

Galatians 6:2 NIV

Carry each other's burdens,
and in this way you will fulfill the law of Christ.

Proverbs 11:25 NIV

A generous person will prosper;
whoever refreshes others will be refreshed.

Luke 5:16 AMP

But Jesus Himself would often slip away to the wilderness
and pray [in seclusion].

Psalm 91:11 KJV

For he shall give his angels charge over thee,
to keep thee in all thy ways.

Grace and Peace, Beloved!

The world typically thinks of being alone in a negative manner. Such aloneness is often associated with having no help, less powerful, being left by oneself, or even abandoned. Moreover, this type of aloneness is involuntary because the person who is alone desires to be in the company of others. This concept of aloneness is akin to emotional loneliness which we prayed through on a previous day in this devotional.

As believers, let's look at being alone in a positive light. Understand that believers harness the power of being alone by simply knowing that we are actually never alone. Father sent the Holy Spirit to abide with us and teach us all things. He reveals to us truths that are hidden for us, not from us. The Holy Spirit opens up heavenly realities to us. The great power that lives in us far outshines the enemy's false power (see 1 John 4:4 KJV). Remember that with him, all things are possible when we believe!

Jesus himself separated himself to spend alone time with the Father; yet, he was not alone during those times. We carry the Holy Spirit on the inside of us. We also have the prayers and support of our brothers and sisters in Christ, even when we are not physically in their presence. Angels are with us to guard and protect us. We are always in good company! How comforting it is to know that we are not alone, not powerless.

Today's Prayer:

Father, I understand the importance of my time with you. Help me if I lose my way and my vision is blurred. I want to see you clearly. I am no longer fixated on the things of this world nor do I place my confidence in this world's system, this world's way of being. I trust you to guide me. I acknowledge and yield to your presence. Help me to honor my time with you. I operate in your power as a child of God because you are living large in me. I am never alone. Thank you, Father, for reviving my heart! In the mighty name of Jesus I pray! Amen.

I am encouraged! You be encouraged, too!

Day 41

Supernatural Help

Psalm 118:8 KJV

It is better to trust in the LORD than to put confidence in man.

Romans 15:13 KJV

Now the God of hope fill you with all joy and peace in believing,
that ye may abound in hope, through the power of the Holy Ghost.

Psalm 31:24 KJV

Be of good courage, and he shall strengthen your heart,
all ye that hope in the LORD.

Grace and Peace, Beloved!

Sometimes we long for someone to be beside us, to lift us up and strengthen us. We may look around for others to encourage us, but it is far better to receive our strengthening from the comforter, the Holy Spirit! His encouragement is perfect and inspires us to go on. If we are out of alignment, he is there to nudge us and help us renew our commitment to the Lord. This support gives us hope, Beloved, that our well-doing is not in vain. We are in this world to make a difference and we will do that, with the Holy Spirit's help.

Christ has already anointed you to fulfill your exact purpose. Yield and listen to the Holy Spirit. He will teach you all things. He will also direct you to certain scriptures pertaining to your specific situation. Encouragement is available to you for the taking!

Today's Prayer:

Father, I thank you for the gift of the Holy Spirit. When I am discouraged, I know you are the remedy. I will always turn to you for encouragement. You are the sovereign God who sits on the throne of my heart. I trust you with my life. In the mighty name of Jesus, I pray! Amen.

I am encouraged! You be encouraged, too!

Part 6
Faith

Day 42

A Sound Belief System

Hebrews 11:6 KJV

But without faith it is impossible to please him: for he that cometh to God must believe that he is, and that he is a rewarder of them that diligently seek him.

James 1:2-4, 23, 24 KJV

2 My brethren, count it all joy when ye fall into divers temptations;

3 Knowing this, that the trying of your faith worketh patience.

4 But let patience have her perfect work, that ye may be perfect and entire, wanting nothing.

23 For if any be a hearer of the word, and not a doer, he is like unto a man beholding his natural face in a glass:

24 For he beholdeth himself, and goeth his way, and straightway forgetteth what manner of man he was.

Mark 11:24 KJV

Therefore I say unto you, What things soever ye desire, when ye pray, believe that ye receive them, and ye shall have them.

Grace and Peace, Beloved!

I am so excited that our Father has us on this faith journey. To get where we are going, to reach our destination, our Father has provided the mirror of his word to sharpen our faith and belief. Do you believe, Beloved? Our steps are ordered by God. However, when we misstep, we can still trust God to put us back on the faith path, the righteous path. He is always with us; even during his times of silence. In order to receive salvation, we first had to believe that God, through his son Jesus, had provided salvation for us! If we can believe in a supernatural transformation of the heart, we can believe for anything. Yes, believing matters!

If you are experiencing a challenge, know that your story is not finished. Soon, you will share a different story - a story of healing, abundance, prosperity, love, happiness, peace, and great joy. Stay in faith and stay focused on God. He make all things right.

Today's Prayer:

Father, I thank you, that even in the thick of trials, I still have faith in you. I am a believer and not a doubter. I rely on your promises and am unshakable in my faith. I am steadfast and unmoved by natural conditions that are contrary to your word. The Holy Spirit is my guide, my standby, and my helper. Giving up is not in my vocabulary. Jesus Christ will never give up on me. He is the only sure foundation in this cold, ever-changing world. He is my solid rock and my anchor. Circumstances may change and people may change, but your word remains true forever. You love me and want the best for me. Thank you for hearing my prayer; I have what I have asked for. In the mighty name of Jesus, I pray! Amen.

I am encouraged! You be encouraged, too!

Day 43

Mustard Seed Faith

Matthew 13:31-32 KJV

31 Another parable put he forth unto them, saying, The kingdom of heaven is like to a grain of mustard seed,

which a man took, and sowed in his field:

32 Which indeed is the least of all seeds: but when it is grown, it is the greatest among herbs, and becometh a tree, so that the birds of the air come and lodge in the branches thereof.

Luke 5:4-6 KJV

4 Now when he had left speaking, he said unto Simon, Launch out into the deep, and let down your nets for a draught.

5 And Simon answering said unto him, Master, we have toiled all the night, and have taken nothing:

nevertheless at thy word I will let down the net.

6 And when they had this done, they inclosed a great multitude of fishes: and their net brake.

Romans 12:3 KJV

For I say, through the grace given unto me, to every man that is among you, not to think of himself more highly than he ought to think; but to think soberly, according as God hath dealt to every man the measure of faith.

Grace and Peace, Beloved!

God doesn't ask for very much. He only requests from us a little faith. Believe! Jesus will help us walk past any fear or unbelief. Little becomes much when we place it in the Master's hands. Just like the tiny mustard seed can grow into a tree up to thirty feet tall with branches nearly as wide (Johansson, 2023), our measure of faith produces results. We have already been given all the faith that we need to bring forth fruit.

Yes, Beloved, hearing the word produces faith. God will perform mighty acts on your behalf. Rejoice now because God loves you. You belong to him. God sees you and is satisfied with you!

Today's Prayer:

Father, I thank you for the measure of faith. I turn over any doubt or unbelief to you. I am moving past those snares to launch out again, in faith. Regardless of fear, I will do it anyway! I will myself to follow your directives. As I step out, you enlighten my righteous path, step by step. Glory to your Name! Thank you for your love towards me. In the mighty name of Jesus, I pray! Amen.

I am encouraged! You be encouraged, too!

Day 44

Active Faith

John 14:15-17 AMP

15 "If you [really] love Me, you will keep and obey My
commandments.
16 And I will ask the Father, and He will give you another Helper
(Comforter, Advocate, Intercessor—Counselor, Strengthener, Standby),
to be with you forever—
17 the Spirit of Truth, whom the world cannot receive [and take to its
heart] because it does not see Him or know Him, but you know Him
because He (the Holy Spirit) remains with you
continually and will be in you.

James 1:25 NKJV

But he who looks into the perfect law of liberty and continues in it,
and is not a forgetful hearer but a doer of the work, this one will be
blessed in what he does.

Isaiah 53:6 NLT

All of us, like sheep, have strayed away. We have left God's paths to
follow our own. Yet the Lord laid on him the sins of us all.

1 Corinthians 3:22-23 NLT

22 whether Paul or Apollos or Peter, or the world, or life and death,
or the present and the future. Everything belongs to you,
23 and you belong to Christ, and Christ belongs to God.

Grace and Peace, Beloved!

God is a good God! He is patient and loving. He is married to the believer! The Holy Spirit has sealed and affirmed all believers as belonging to God. We can rest assured that our relationship with the Father is solid.

I mean, I've known him from a child. I gave my life to him at a young age. But looking back at the relationship, I only saw him as my savior in the context of saving me from one trouble to the next. I did not know him as the lover of my soul. I knew the word but bore no fruit. I did not fully grasp the enormity of what salvation really meant. I straddled the fence for years before I totally surrendered to him as my Lord. Bless God! He followed me until I could follow him. He pursued me; he wanted me. I love him for that!

I want to encourage you, today. If you are in sin, allow the Lord to change your mind. Listen to the voice of the Holy Spirit and go in that direction! Do not allow your heart to be hardened. Your love for Jesus Christ will be evident through the manner in which you live. Allow your belief, your words, and your actions to align! Let us not just hear the word but do the word!

Today's Prayer:

Father, thank you for keeping my heart soft and receptive to your leading. I am a doer of the word and I bear much fruit. My beliefs, words, and actions are in alignment with your will. I receive the totality of salvation provided to me through Jesus Christ. In the mighty name of Jesus, I pray! Amen.

I am encouraged! You be encouraged, too!

Day 45

Faith Is Now

Hebrews 6:18-19 KJV

*18 That by two immutable things, in which it was impossible for God
to lie, we might have a strong consolation, who have fled for refuge to lay
hold upon the hope set before us:
19 Which hope we have as an anchor of the soul, both sure and
stedfast, and which entereth into that within the veil;*

1 John 5:4 KJV

*For whatsoever is born of God overcometh the world:
and this is the victory that overcometh the world, even our faith.*

Hebrews 11:1 KJV

*Now faith is the substance of things hoped for,
the evidence of things not seen.*

Grace and Peace, Beloved!

We have a secure future in Jesus Christ. He is our hope. Faith is the material that assures us right now that we will see him face to face one day.

Likewise, all good things come from our Father - originating from the richness of his grace and the kindness of his character. Right now, we are blessed with all spiritual blessings in heavenly places. Because we have all spiritual blessings, we can pull those blessings into the earthly realm. Faith assures us that we have those blessings. Faith and hope work together. Hope is in the future, but faith is now.

I have come through seasons of dryness when it seemed like everything was going wrong. In those times, faith sustained me until I could see manifestation of what I hoped for. I encourage you to engage your faith today; put in in gear. I am standing with you as you anticipate the manifestation of all for which you are believing.

Today's Prayer:

Lord Jesus, all I have is you! You plus nothing is all I will ever need. You are my hope. I have faith in you. I am blessed because of you. I receive those blessings for myself, my loved ones, my friends, and my family. Give me patience and endurance as I anticipate the end result of my faith and prayers. No matter what is happening in my life or seems to be going wrong, you love me. That is an immutable fact. I know you are helping me to rest in your love. In the mighty name of Jesus, I pray! Amen.

I am encouraged! You be encouraged, too!

Day 46

The Shield of Faith

Ephesians 6:11 KJV

Put on the whole armor of God, that you may be able to stand against the wiles of the devil.

I John 5:4 KJV

For whatsoever is born of God overcometh the world: and this is the victory that overcometh the world, even our faith.

Psalm 144:1 KJV

Blessed be the Lord my strength which teacheth my hands to war, and my fingers to fight:

Grace and Peace, Beloved!

Our King has given us amazing grace! We have everything we need to rise up and stand today. He placed this living word in our hands which is more powerful than any two-edged sword.

He has given us the victory, Beloved, through our faith. Yes, our faith is a conquering weapon. No weapon formed against us shall prosper.

Whom shall we fear? We only fear God which means we give him the love and respect He deserves. He has given us faith, peace, joy, and love. Let's be of good cheer because we know we are children of the King of Kings! To know we are his children, lightens our steps; it causes us to skip, hop, leap, and dance for joy!

Today's Prayer: A Prayer of Exaltation

Oh Hallelujah! Father, I thank you that you fight my battles. I cry Daddy, Abba, Father! I know I am safe under the shadow of your wings, Daddy. You are mighty to save and demons flee at the mention of your name. My weapons are not carnal but mighty through you, to the pulling down of strongholds. I raise my shield of faith today in Jesus' name! The battle is not mine, but yours. In the mighty name of Jesus, I pray! Amen.

I am encouraged! You be encouraged, too!

Day 47

Uncommon Faith

Romans 10:14-15, 17 KJV

14 How then shall they call on him in whom they have not believed? and how shall they believe in him of whom they have not heard? and how shall they hear without a preacher?

15 And how shall they preach, except they be sent? as it is written, How beautiful are the feet of them that preach the gospel of peace, and bring glad tidings of good things!

17 So then faith cometh by hearing, and hearing by the word of God.

Mark 11:22-24 KJV

22 And Jesus answering saith unto them, Have faith in God.

23 For verily I say unto you, That whosoever shall say unto this mountain, Be thou removed, and be thou cast into the sea; and shall not doubt in his heart, but shall believe that those things which he saith shall come to pass; he shall have whatsoever he saith.

24 Therefore I say unto you, What things soever ye desire, when ye pray, believe that ye receive them, and ye shall have them.

Proverbs 27:17 NIV

As iron sharpens iron, so one person sharpens another.

Romans 3:4 KJV

God forbid: yea, let God be true, but every man a liar; as it is written, That thou mightest be justified in thy sayings, and mightest overcome when thou art judged.

Grace and Peace, Beloved!

The scriptures are very clear that faith comes by hearing the word preached and taught. It is so important to be a part of a church and ministry that teaches and preaches the word of God. The Father knows that this type of fellowship and accountability will increase and sharpen our faith. We will then be absolutely able to walk by faith and not by our physical senses.

In my personal journey, I am outright refusing any unbelief. I know that faith is a constant; the Lord does not change. Regardless of what the situation looks like, I believe the word that tells me to ask, believe, and receive. I am encouraging myself today, Beloved! I am confident that my Father fulfills all of his promises.

Today is the day to crush any doubtful thoughts that try to align with probabilities or statistics. For example, the doctor's report may give a diagnosis and prognosis, but the higher law is that you are healed. Perhaps, you have received a bill in the mail that you are unable to pay. The higher law is that our loving Father supplies all that you need. No probability, statistic, or man-crafted assessment can stand against the knowledge of Jesus Christ.

117

Today's Prayer:

Father, I thank you for placing me in a body of believers with whom I can fellowship and be sharpened. As I hear the word of God preached and taught, my faith grows stronger. Lord, you have instructed me to walk by faith and not by my physical senses. Give me the grace, Lord, to have fearless faith.

Thank you for hearing me, today. I totally depend on you and expect manifestation of my prayers. The only thing that matters is you King Jesus. In the mighty name of Jesus, I pray! Amen.

I am encouraged! You be encouraged, too!

Part 7
Strength

Day 48

God Is on My Side

Jude 1:24-25 KJV

24 Now unto him that is able to keep you from falling, and to present you faultless before the presence of his glory with exceeding joy,

25 To the only wise God our Saviour, be glory and majesty, dominion and power, both now and ever. Amen.

2 Corinthians 10:4-5 KJV

4 (For the weapons of our warfare are not carnal, but mighty through God to the pulling down of strong holds;)

5 Casting down imaginations, and every high thing that exalteth itself against the knowledge of God, and bringing into captivity every thought to the obedience of Christ;

Psalm 121:3 NLT

He will not let you stumble; the one who watches over you will not slumber.

Grace and Peace, Beloved!

As we work on our spiritual development, the devil seeks to place things in our path to alter our future. He puts stumbling blocks in our pathway to cause us to fall. The good news is that our Father is able to keep us from falling! Let's renew our minds to that revelation.

Pull down the strongholds and thought patterns that go against the knowledge of Jesus Christ. Expose the adversary for the liar that he is. Ask for wisdom today; God grants it liberally when we ask. Remember, Father is for you, not against you.

Today's Prayer:

Father God, I decree and declare that you are my rock; you are my strong tower. You have equipped me with salvation and your right hand establishes me as a victor in battle. The Psalmist cried, "Thou hast also given me the necks of mine enemies; that I might destroy them that hate me (Psalm 18:40 KJV)". I thank you, Father, that my enemies are already defeated. Cause me to pursue and overtake them until they are wounded and consumed falling at my feet never to rise again. Life is so much easier when I take one day at a time. In the mighty name of Jesus I pray! Amen.

I am encouraged! You be encouraged, too!

Day 49

God Strengthens Me

Matthew 6:34 KJV

Take therefore no thought for the morrow: for the morrow shall take thought for the things of itself. Sufficient unto the day is the evil thereof.

2 Corinthians 6:2 KJV

(For he saith, I have heard thee in a time accepted, and in the day of salvation have I succoured thee: behold, now is the accepted time; behold, now is the day of salvation.)

Psalm 31:24 KJV

Be of good courage, and he shall strengthen your heart, all ye that hope in the LORD.

Grace and Peace, Beloved!

The words of Jesus regarding taking no thought for tomorrow are exploding with wisdom. This one directive is loaded with insight on how to manage our lives. The Father, the Son, and the Holy Spirit are very purposeful. Their language is precise and designed to communicate multiple messages, sometimes within just a few words. In this passage, we can see the benefit of casting aside worry, trusting in Jesus, prioritizing our immediate concerns, learning how to focus, and the importance of not "taking the thought." The power to influence and change our destiny begins with today, with the now.

When the enemy tries to bombard your mind with thoughts of past failures, don't take the thought. When the enemy tries to tell you that you are weak, speak aloud that, "I am strong because the strength of Christ is perfect in my weakness." The purpose of his strength is to strengthen you when you are weak. You can replace your strength with his strength. Today is the day of salvation which means restoration, preservation, and deliverance from peril or danger is here now. Be strengthened today!

Today's Prayer:

Father, I thank you that I can rely on your strength to support me in times of weakness. I need not worry about yesterday's inadequacies or tomorrow's demands. Today is the day of salvation. I have an earnest expectation that you have already arrived in my tomorrow and will meet me there with all sufficiency. Yes, I have hope. I stand in your grace. In the mighty name of Jesus, I pray! Amen.

I am encouraged! You be encouraged, too!

Day 50

Perfect Strength

2 Corinthians 12:9 KJV

And he said unto me, My grace is sufficient for thee: for my strength is made perfect in weakness. Most gladly therefore will I rather glory in my infirmities, that the power of Christ may rest upon me.

Exodus 15:11 KJV

Who is like unto thee, O Lord, among the gods? who is like thee, glorious in holiness, fearful in praises, doing wonders?

Psalm 24:7-8 KJV

7 Lift up your heads, O ye gates; and be ye lift up, ye everlasting doors; and the King of glory shall come in.
8 Who is this King of glory? The LORD strong and mighty, the LORD mighty in battle.

Grace and Peace, Beloved!

There is nobody like the Lord. His strength is perfect when ours is depleted. He is our victory. As our bodies need constant oxygen to survive, we need him every hour, every minute, every second. The battle is real; yet, he is more real. In battle, he is with us. Every victory won is because of him, the Lord who is invincible in battle.

I am on this battlefield, too. I have realized that everything I will ever need in life will flow from my intimate relationship with Jesus. As I grow and mature in the faith, satan's attacks become stronger. As the saying goes, "New levels, new devils." That's my signal that I am doing damage to the kingdom of darkness. It is so comforting to know that the King is with me and has defeated the enemy on my behalf. I do not have to be strong on my own, by myself.

You have the victory. Keep your eyes on Jesus, you victorious water walker! All is well with you.

Today's Prayer:

Father, I thank you that your goodness and mercy follow me always. Holy Spirit, lead me today because I want to walk with purpose, placing my feet exactly where you instruct me on my righteous path. I put my trust in you! You are my source of strength and victory. Your strength is perfect, enduring, and unfailing.

I receive your boldness in the midst of battle. I stand and lift up your holy name. I thank you for all types of favor, with you and with man, flowing into my life today. That name, Jesus, is anointed to produce results. Your word alone stands true in the midst of anything I face. Thank you for answered prayers today. I expect great things knowing all good things come from you. In the mighty name of Jesus, I pray! Amen.

I am encouraged! You be encouraged, too!

Day 51

Keep Going

Philippians 1:6 KJV

Being confident of this very thing, that he which hath begun a good work in you will perform it until the day of Jesus Christ:

Matthew 11:28-29 KJV

28 Come unto me, all ye that labour and are heavy laden, and I will give you rest.
29 Take my yoke upon you, and learn of me; for I am meek and lowly in heart: and ye shall find rest unto your souls.
30 For my yoke is easy, and my burden is light.

Psalm 138:7 NIV

Though I walk in the midst of trouble, you preserve my life. You stretch out your hand against the anger of my foes; with your right hand you save me.

Grace and Peace, Beloved!

I am a witness that we don't always see that his yoke is easy. In fact, sometimes life may feel harder when we have made the decision to stand for righteousness. Because of our stance, satan makes it his business to pick on us. He taunts us and has the nerve to laugh and yell, "Where is your God?" Even in the midst of harassment from the enemy, our Father is with us and the Holy Spirit is moving. We remain unbothered by satan's tactics.

When God seems silent, keep seeking him and doing the right things! Pay attention to the "still" small voice inside of you. That voice points us to Jesus and the word. You are okay. You are right where you're supposed to be. You're not too early; you're not too late; you are right on time. All is well with you.

Today's Prayer:

Father, I thank you that no matter where I am in life, you are with me. Your word and the Holy Spirit guide and comfort me. I am neither dismayed nor distressed. I trust the process. I am a work in progress standing on your promise that you will complete the good work that you began in me. Your promises are sure, reliable, dependable, trustworthy, and true. In the mighty name of Jesus, I pray! Amen.

I am encouraged! You be encouraged, too!

Day 52

Power for Action

Colossians 1:11 NLT
We also pray that you will be strengthened with all his glorious power so you will have all the endurance and patience you need. May you be filled with joy,

Psalm 18:1-2 KJV
1 I will love thee, O LORD, my strength.
2 The LORD is my rock, and my fortress, and my deliverer;
my God, my strength, in whom I will trust; my buckler, and the horn of my salvation, and my high tower.

Psalm 18:33-34 AMPC
33 He makes my feet like hinds' feet [able to stand firmly or make progress on the dangerous heights of testing and trouble];
He sets me securely upon my high places.
34 He teaches my hands to war, so that my arms can bend a bow of bronze.

Daniel 11:32 KJV

And such as do wickedly against the covenant shall he corrupt by flatteries: but the people that do know their God shall be strong, and do exploits.

Grace and Peace, Beloved!

As children of God, members of the royal family, we have immeasurable power. That power is not in our own strength but in the strength of the Anointed One. Once we have prayed and received instructions from the Holy Spirit, we have the power to act and do great things that bring glory to God. We do not walk in fear but walk in the authority that Christ has given us.

Walk in your power today! Go and be great. With God on your side, who can oppose you?

Today's Prayer:

Father, I thank you that you have strengthened me with your supernatural power. I can conquer armies with the unbeatable army of angels fighting on my behalf. I can leap over walls! You are my God who makes my path perfect. You make my feet as hind's feet, giving me stability; I stand securely. You teach me how to fight this good fight of faith. I am strong and do great exploits. Thank you for being my rock and my fortified tower. In the mighty name of Jesus, I pray! Amen.

I am encouraged! You be encouraged, too!

Day 53

Anointed to Make Spiritual Progress

Psalm 84:5,7 KJV

5 Blessed is the man whose strength is in thee; in whose heart are the ways of them.

7 They go from strength to strength, every one of them in Zion appeareth before God.

Hebrews 12:2 KJV

Looking unto Jesus the author and finisher of our faith; who for the joy that was set before him endured the cross, despising the shame, and is set down at the right hand of the throne of God.

2 Corinthians 3:18 KJV

But we all, with open face beholding as in a glass the glory of the Lord, are changed into the same image from glory to glory, even as by the Spirit of the Lord.

Grace and Peace, Beloved!

The Holy Spirit is here to help us make spiritual progress - moving us from one degree of God's glory to another. If we look to our natural selves, we are imperfect. However, God looks at us through the lens of Jesus and all he has done. The work is finished. The blood work is complete. We are perfect in Jesus Christ. God sees the Savior, not us. Thank God for Jesus!

I have found that God is revealing much to me regarding my struggles. The Master Deliverer is at work helping me to shed anything that does not look like him. I stand in what Christ has done and walk freely in his grace.

Receive his grace today! His grace is sufficient. Don't feed your weakness, Beloved. Whatever we entertain or feed gains strength. Instead, feed your spirit the truth of God's word that you are a reflection of God's splendor. Cast aside thoughts of imperfection, shame, weakness, and fear and lay them at the feet of Jesus. Jesus has born the shame on your behalf. You never have to walk that way again. Continue in the faith and welcome his pruning as needed. Jesus himself is responsible for finishing and polishing you. He is not done with you so allow him to refine you until your outward display matches his exact image. Remember, no shame and no fear!

I encourage you today to do what might feel uncomfortable to you. Do not run from God but run to him. Besides, he already knows all about you. There is no where you can hide from him. The Holy Spirit is always with you and will help you!

Today's Prayer:

Holy Spirit, I thank you for taking me by the hand and helping me to lay aside any weights that would hinder me finishing this race. Father, I am so grateful that you see me through the blood of Jesus. I am perfect in your eyes. I yield to your polishing and refining. Thank you for caring for me so beautifully. In the mighty name of Jesus, I pray! Amen.

I am encouraged! You be encouraged,too!

Day 54

Times of Refreshing

Isaiah 44:3 KJV

For I will pour water upon him that is thirsty, and floods upon the dry ground: I will pour my spirit upon thy seed, and my blessing upon thine offspring:

Psalm 68:9 NLT

You sent abundant rain, O God, to refresh the weary land.

Joel 2:23 NLT

Rejoice, you people of Jerusalem! Rejoice in the Lord your God! For the rain he sends demonstrates his faithfulness. Once more the autumn rains will come, as well as the rains of spring.

Grace and Peace, Beloved!

The fragrance of rain brings joy. There is something calming about this delightful, earthy scent. It can evoke childhood memories, invite one to go outside to dance and splash, and inspire companies to replicate its allure in certain products. Rain itself refreshes the earth and causes plants to grow. It symbolizes healing and cleansing. Let's ask the Father to let it rain today. We anticipate a rain of glory, a rain of his presence, a rain of transformation, a rain of his peace! When we are worn, we need a refreshing!

As you anticipate your time of refreshing, remember to just enjoy that time. Do not think about the next task on your list. Allow the Father to saturate you today.

Today's Prayer:

Father, I receive the rain. I am refreshed, cleansed, and healed. You saturate my very being today. I allow you to minister to me. In the mighty name of Jesus, I pray! Amen.

I am encouraged! You be encouraged, too!

Part 8
Count It All Joy

Day 55

Good Trials

Ecclesiastes 3:1, 11 KJV

1 To every thing there is a season, and a time to every purpose under the heaven:

11 He hath made every thing beautiful in his time: also he hath set the world in their heart, so that no man can find out the work that God maketh from the beginning to the end.

1 Corinthians 10:13 KJV

There hath no temptation taken you but such as is common to man: but God is faithful, who will not suffer you to be tempted above that ye are able; but will with the temptation also make a way to escape, that ye may be able to bear it.

2 Corinthians 4:17 KJV

For our light affliction, which is but for a moment, worketh for us a far more exceeding and eternal weight of glory;

Grace and Peace, Beloved!

Allow me to work this message into your day. Not every challenge and problem is necessarily bad for us. Here is what I mean. Some situations we encounter will be difficult and painful, but in the long run, that storm will be for our good. That challenge will make us stronger. Remember, we love the Lord and the promise is that all things work together, in concert, for our benefit! Most importantly, the Lord loves us.

So come on! Believe that crisis is going to work out for your good! Some of you may even be sick right now but will recover in such a way that we can see nothing but the hand of God! You will experience a miracle. God's glory will be seen in your deliverance. Perhaps you have had seemingly important plans disrupted only to find out that the disruption is leading you to a better plan, a better destination. Perhaps your plans have been delayed. Just think of the delay as God's way of saying, "Not yet. I have something better for you; I have a different time." Whatever it may be, God holds you in the palm of his hand.

Today's Prayer:

Father, I know that you are not confined to my expectation of when things should happen. I lay every care about timing at the feet of Jesus. Father, I trust you with my heart and know that all of your plans are good for me. I receive your patience and resist any anxiety about your perfect plan for my life. Thank you for your enduring kindness and mercy towards me. In the mighty name of Jesus I pray! Amen.

I am encouraged! You be encouraged, too!

Day 56

How to Endure Suffering

Romans 8:18 KJV

For I reckon that the sufferings of this present time are not worthy to be compared with the glory which shall be revealed in us.

Psalm 61:2 KJV

From the end of the earth will I cry unto thee,
when my heart is overwhelmed:
lead me to the rock that is higher than I.

1 Peter 5:10 KJV

But the God of all grace, who hath called us unto his eternal glory by Christ Jesus, after that ye have suffered a while, make you perfect, stablish, strengthen, settle you.

Grace and Peace, Beloved!

It is so reassuring to know that our present suffering pales in comparison to the glory which will be revealed in us, sons and daughters of the Most High. In the current moment, suffering may appear insurmountable and overwhelming. We find comfort in knowing that we can look to our Rock, our Strong Tower, our Deliverer for liberation from trouble.

Beloved, when you are experiencing suffering on any level, remember the extreme suffering that Jesus endured to bring us into the fold and into the family of God. Shifting into that perspective certainly brings about profound thanksgiving. We are eternally grateful for the immeasurable gift of the Anointed One, Jesus Christ, who fully reconciled us to God.

Today's Prayer:

Father, when my heart feels overwhelmed, I quickly look to you and embrace your inexhaustible love for me. I set my will to not allow the distractions of the world to choke the word! I do not forget your word; rather, I retain it and am a doer of your word. I am moved to action by your word. Your word is my hope, and I will continue to go towards my help. My help is in your living word! As I worship you and lift you up, I am strengthened and bathed in joy. You are my, God, in whom I trust. You fill my cup completely until it overflows. In the mighty name of Jesus, I pray! Amen.

I am encouraged! You be encouraged, too!

Day 57

Not Forsaken

Isaiah 40:28 KJV

Hast thou not known? hast thou not heard, that the everlasting God, the LORD, the Creator of the ends of the earth, fainteth not, neither is weary? there is no searching of his understanding.

Psalm 121:4-5 KJV

4 Behold, he that keepeth Israel shall neither slumber nor sleep.

5 The LORD is thy keeper: the LORD is thy shade upon thy right hand.

Psalm 37:25 KJV

I have been young, and now am old; yet have I not seen the righteous forsaken, nor his seed begging bread.

Grace and Peace, Beloved!

Sometimes we may feel forsaken and forgotten. We may feel like God is not hearing us, and he is nowhere to be found. Then the still small voice of the Comforter brings remembrance to our spirit that the Father never sleeps nor slumbers; he never grows weary or tired.

No matter how weak our faith or how deep the pain, he has not hidden his face, Beloved. He always hears us. In fact, in Isaiah we read,

> *And it shall come to pass, that before they call, I will answer; and*
> *while they are yet speaking, I will hear*
> Isaiah 65:24 KJV

We may wonder why he has not rescued us if he hears us. Why has the pain (situation, challenge, trial, attack) not subsided? Let's stretch our faith for a moment and think outside the box.

We know God hears us; he is omnipotent and omniscient. We serve a God who is present everywhere, all-knowing and all-seeing. Perhaps it's not a matter of him rushing to bring us out. Maybe it's not about just obliterating the problem. Could it be about him transforming us? Could it be about him bringing us into a closer position with him?

I mean we are on our knees now. We are desperately calling out to him. We are realizing we need him. We are understanding that he is Lord of all. Through all that ever comes our way, we trust him to be our redeemer and the lifter of our heads. We are depending again.

Today's Prayer:

Father, I know that you are sustaining me through everything. You rebuild me and strengthen me. When I am delivered, everyone will know that it was your hand at work. People will be astounded and exclaim, "Look at what the Lord has done. This is his great work. Isn't it marvelous?" I believe and declare that all things are working for my good. In the mighty name of Jesus, I pray! Amen.

I am encouraged! You be encouraged, too!

Day 58

Storms

Mark 4:39 KJV

And he arose, and rebuked the wind, and said unto the sea,
Peace, be still.
And the wind ceased, and there was a great calm.

Revelation 12:11 KJV

And they overcame him by the blood of the Lamb,
and by the word of their testimony;
and they loved not their lives unto the death.

Psalm 107:29 KJV

He maketh the storm a calm, so that the waves thereof are still.

Grace and Peace, Beloved!

We are all on this journey called life. We are on our way to the other side. In this journey, storms will come, Beloved. Some may ask why. Well, some storms come to test our faith, but most storms arise simply because we live in a fallen world. Storms do not discriminate. White, black, brown, yellow, big or small, rich or poor, whether you know Jesus or not, in this journey we will all face storms. As believers under the authority of Jesus Christ, we have the power to command storms to cease. Yet, when they don't cease, we have the grace to endure, to remain calm and steady. We can survive and overcome any obstacle because the Anointed One lives on the inside of us. The blood of Jesus coupled with our testimony (our declaration of the word and how the word has freed us) positions us to see victory.

I have encountered many storms in my life. These situations have deepened my trust in the One who has delivered me from all of my afflictions, made miraculous ways of escape, calmed all my fears, and rescued me from trouble.

I encourage you to speak aloud the prayer below. In the personal space, note a testimony of God's goodness regarding a storm in your life. Share the good news with someone else. You have no idea how much your testimony will impact others.

Today's Prayer:

Father, I thank you that the blood of Jesus has made me free. I am victorious in you. You are on my side; therefore, none can be against me. By your grace, I speak to every storm, every irritation, every challenge in my life and command them to cease. You anointed me to speak life and to endure as I await manifestation of these prayers. In the mighty name of Jesus, I pray! Amen.

I am encouraged! You be encouraged, too!

Personal space to note testimony:

———————————————————————————————

———————————————————————————————

———————————————————————————————

———————————————————————————————

Day 59

Patience

1 Peter 5:4 AMP

And when the Chief Shepherd (Christ) appears, you will receive the [conqueror's] unfading crown of glory.

James 1:12 KJV

Blessed is the man that endureth temptation: for when he is tried, he shall receive the crown of life, which the Lord hath promised to them that love him.

1 Corinthians 15:58 KJV

Therefore, my beloved brethren, be ye stedfast, unmoveable, always abounding in the work of the Lord, forasmuch as ye know that your labour is not in vain in the Lord.

Grace and Peace, Beloved!

Remaining steadfast under trial is not so easy in our natural abilities. The pain and suffering may be great, but, oh, an even greater award awaits us. The scriptures tell us that when Jesus appears, we shall receive the "unfading crown of glory (1 Peter 5:4 AMP)." What a glorious day that will be when we stand before Jesus and receive a reward that eclipses the trials we have endured. On that day, our suffering will be no more. Jesus will wipe away every tear. We will bask in the pure joy of seeing how everything has come together. The revelation we know now will be complete as we receive our crowns.

So be of good cheer, Beloved! Hold your head up high and encourage yourself in the Lord. You are a king; you are a queen. You are of the royal family, and all is well with you.

Today's Prayer:

Father, I thank you for the patience to endure various tests and trials. Patience is bringing me into full spiritual maturity. Jesus, when you appear, I will be exactly like you. I am a child of God and have nothing to fear. In the mighty name of Jesus, I pray! Amen.

I am encouraged! You be encouraged, too!

Day 60

Stir Up Joy

Nehemiah 8:10 KJV

Then he said unto them, Go your way, eat the fat, and drink the sweet, and send portions unto them for whom nothing is prepared: for this day is holy unto our LORD: neither be ye sorry; for the joy of the LORD is your strength.

John 16:24 NIV

Until now you have not asked for anything in my name. Ask and you will receive, and your joy will be complete.

Proverbs 17:22 VOICE

A joy-filled heart is curative balm, but a broken spirit hurts all the way to the bone.

Luke 22:19 KJV

And he took bread, and gave thanks, and brake it, and gave unto them, saying, This is my body which is given for you: this do in remembrance of me.

Grace and Peace, Beloved!

We all desire happiness. Such a desire is reasonable, but that is not always our reality. Instead of happiness, let's pursue joy! The joy of the Lord will surpass our natural understanding. When we have pure joy, happiness will follow. Seek joy from the Lord, and you will be strengthened. One beautiful method by which to stir up our joy is through remembrance.

Think about all that he has done for you. Go to your memories. Memories are an effective means to stir up your joy. Do you remember the words Jesus spoke to his disciples while leading them in communion before his death?

Luke 22:19b (KJV)
This is my body which is given for you:
this do in remembrance of me.

Jesus was teaching them the power of remembrance. He knew they would feel sadness at his death. Yet, instead of grief, he encouraged them to pull out the memories of every miracle, every healing, every exorcism, every awe-inspiring moment of their time together. In other words, remember who I am, remember what I came to do, remember I accomplished it all, and remember I love you. At that time, the disciples probably did not fully understand the scope of all they had witnessed. Jesus, in his omnipresence, spoke into their future.

Remember all that our Lord has done, Beloved, and stir up your joy.

Today's Prayer:

Jesus, I thank you for complete salvation. I remember your sacrifice for me. Reminding myself of your astonishing love rekindles my joy. I am full of your joy today. In the mighty name of Jesus, I pray! Amen.

I am encouraged! You be encouraged, too!

Day 61

Press Into Joy

Philippians 4:4 KJV

Rejoice in the Lord always: and again I say, Rejoice.

Psalm 16:11 KJV

Thou wilt shew me the path of life: in thy presence is fulness of joy;
at thy right hand there are pleasures for evermore.

Psalm 118:24 KJV

This is the day which the LORD hath made;
we will rejoice and be glad in it.

John 16:33 KJV

These things I have spoken unto you, that in me ye might have peace.
In the world ye shall have tribulation:
but be of good cheer; I have overcome the world.

Grace and Peace, Beloved!

We have another day to rejoice because Father woke us up! Whether we are experiencing pain or pleasure, both are invitations to prayer and praise. We are growing in the Lord, and we gain confidence in him because we have experienced his love. The Father had our backs yesterday; he is here today, tomorrow, and forevermore. We are never alone because God, our Father, sits on the throne. Great is His faithfulness towards us!

Keep your relationship with him active and dwell in his presence all day. There is no time for running away; always run to him. Grab your ReJoy. It's your strength. Come on now! It is time for change with no fear. Tomorrow will take care of itself.

Today's Prayer:

Father, I receive your supernatural strength and joy. In the places where I may feel weak, you are my strength. Those are the prime places where you show up to remind me that I can do nothing without you. You are never weary, never worn, never weak and I can always draw from you. I go about my day rejoicing over your extravagant love for me. In the mighty name of Jesus I pray! Amen.

I am encouraged! You be encouraged, too!

Day 62

War from a Place of Joy!

Isaiah 12:3 KJV

Therefore with joy shall ye draw water out of the wells of salvation.

John 7:38 KJV

He that believeth on me, as the scripture hath said, out of his belly shall flow rivers of living water.

Zephaniah 3:17 KJV

The Lord thy God in the midst of thee is mighty;
he will save, he will rejoice over thee with joy;
he will rest in his love, he will joy over thee with singing.

Grace and Peace, Beloved!

We know that trials and tribulations will come. Those times of testing and attacks from the enemy are not the problem. We are in this world system but not of it. We accept that tests will come. The real problem begins when we choose no longer to believe internally. Strength in battle is determined by what's going on in our minds.

153

The good news is that regardless of what we are going through, God desires that we keep our joy internally. There should be a well of joy that constantly springs up from the inside.

Here is the remedy. Choose Joy! Smile for yourself beloved because God himself smiles and sings over you. Bring up those rivers of living water; gain confidence in your hope in the Lord. I don't care how unstable your life may look, stay stable internally and keep your mind focused on the Savior, the one who saves totally and completely.

Today's Prayer:

Holy Spirit, help me to remain stable internally as I keep my heart set on you. Help me to remain in a place of internal victory! That internal victory must express itself outwardly. The joy of the Lord is my strength. I rest and withdraw from the wells of salvation. Father, thank you for strength and restoration of my joy today. In the name of Jesus I pray! Amen.

I am encouraged! You be encouraged, too!

Day 63

Morning Joy

Psalm 34:19 KJV

Many are the afflictions of the righteous: but the LORD delivereth him out of them all.

Psalm 30:5 KJV

For his anger endureth but a moment; in his favour is life: weeping may endure for a night, but joy cometh in the morning.

James 1:2-4 KJV

2 My brethren, count it all joy when ye fall into divers temptations;
3 Knowing this, that the trying of your faith worketh patience.
4 But let patience have her perfect work, that ye may be perfect and entire, wanting nothing.

Grace and Peace, Beloved!

In this journey of life, we experience good times, hard times, highs, and lows. As believers we are not immune to hardships. In fact, sometimes it seems that our experiences are more difficult than those experiences of nonbelievers. The scripture tells us that we will have many afflictions. However, the Lord always delivers us. When we examine Psalm 34:19 (KJV) more closely, the sentence structure alone places the emphasis on "but the Lord delivereth him out of them all." When two thoughts are connected by the word, "but," the second thought practically dismisses the first. So let's focus on the deliverance, Beloved, not the affliction.

I have realized that when I face problems or pain, it does not mean that the Lord loves me less then anyone else. I am a witness that joy really does come in the morning! The morning may be symbolic or may even be an actual morning once I have rested and allowed the Holy Spirit to minister to me in my sleep.

Today's devotion is not to discourage you at all, Beloved. On the contrary, it is here to lift you up. Jesus does not exempt us from problems or pain, but he does promise to deliver us.

Today's Prayer:

Father, I thank you that I find joy in you. I allow patience to work perfectly in me, maturing me, and helping me to navigate this life with grace. I am of good cheer; Jesus has already overcome the cares of this world on my behalf. In the mighty name of Jesus, I pray! Amen.

I am encouraged! You be encouraged, too!

Part 9
Prayer &
Spiritual Warfare

Day 64

A Prayer Posture That Produces Results

Luke 18:1 AMP

Now Jesus was telling the disciples a parable to make the point that at all times they ought to pray and not give up and lose heart,

James 5:16 AMP

Therefore, confess your sins to one another [your false steps, your offenses], and pray for one another, that you may be healed and restored. The heartfelt and persistent prayer of a righteous man (believer) can accomplish much [when put into action and made effective by God—it is dynamic and can have tremendous power].

Romans 12:12 KJV

Rejoicing in hope; patient in tribulation; continuing instant in prayer;

Mark 11:24 KJV

Therefore I say unto you, What things soever ye desire, when ye pray, believe that ye receive them, and ye shall have them.

Grace and Peace, Beloved!

As believers, we have been called to pray consistently and persistently! This call is not an option; it's a commandment from Jesus himself. Jesus tells us to pray and to never lose heart because prayer is our lifeline.

One of my prayers for the body of Christ is that we operate in a full, consistent, productive prayer life. There have been days when I, personally, have felt low and like my joy was gone. Let me tell you, the Holy Spirit on the inside of me does not allow me to ever give up! Emotions are temporary; my life with God is eternal.

Now don't get me wrong, Beloved. There is a difference between praying persistently and having a long prayer session. Effectual prayer is not constrained by the clock. Allow the Holy Spirit to guide you regarding the length of time. Additionally, you may not be able to get on your knees, necessarily. The point is that you do not give up on God; you do not stop believing, talking with him, and listening to him! Opportunity for prayer is constant as we go about our day.

Today's Prayer:

Father, thank you for instructing me to saturate my life with prayer. I know that I can always talk with you. My prayer time is productive and produces results as I pray your word. As I pray in my secret closet, my personal space, you reward me openly with the manifestation of all that I have prayed. In the mighty name of Jesus, I pray! Amen.

I am encouraged! You be encouraged, too!

Day 65

Pray Without Ceasing

1 Thessalonians 5:17 KJV

Pray without ceasing.

Matthew 7:11 KJV

If ye then, being evil, know how to give good gifts unto your children, how much more shall your Father which is in heaven give good things to them that ask him?

Ephesians 6:18 AMPC

Pray at all times (on every occasion, in every season) in the Spirit, with all [manner of] prayer and entreaty. To that end keep alert and watch with strong purpose and perseverance, interceding in behalf of all the saints (God's consecrated people).

Grace and Peace, Beloved!

Prayer destroys the kingdom of darkness. We will not cease to pray for we know it's power. We will not faint! Our Father hears us as we pray and answers before we call. We will continue to pray at all times, not just for ourselves and our needs, but for the body of believers everywhere. God always answers; our part is to believe!

I challenge you, Beloved! Ask someone how you can agree with them in prayer today.

Today's Prayer:

Father, I thank you that you hear me every time I pray. Your word does not return void but accomplishes its exact purpose. I thank you for meeting every need that I have and allowing me to be a blessing to others. I agree with my loved ones that their needs are met as well. You are perfecting that good work that you began in me. I cooperate with your call. In the mighty name of Jesus, I pray! Amen.

I am encouraged! You be encouraged, too!

Day 66

Praying for the Heart of God

Psalm 51:10 KJV

Create in me a clean heart, O God;
and renew a right spirit within me.

Acts 13:22 KJV

And when he had removed him, he raised up unto them David to be
their king; to whom also he gave their testimony, and said,
I have found David the son of Jesse, a man after mine own heart,
which shall fulfill all my will.

Matthew 5:8 KJV

Blessed are the pure in heart: for they shall see God.

Grace and Peace, Beloved!

I love the example of David being a man after God's own heart. It gives me courage to know that, like us, he had flaws. He had mess and caused mess too, but I believe he received much favor because he was quick to repent once he realized and acknowledged the error of his ways.

David was God-centered and longed to operate from the pure, undefiled heart of God.

God is no respecter of persons. He loves us just as he loved David. God was not pleased with David's sins, but He loved David's heart! Remember, that God is omniscient, all-knowing. He knew David when he was a young lad tending sheep. He also knew that David would make mistakes yet anointed him to kingship. As Acts 13:22 (KJV) shows us, the Father knew that David would fulfill **ALL** his will. So it is with you, Beloved!

Today's Prayer:

Father, give me a heart like David's and help me to fulfill all your will for my life. I honor and respect your heart, Father. In my intimate time with you, convict me and convince me of any attitudes and behaviors that are not like you. I yield myself to repent quickly meaning I turn away from those destructive patterns and live differently. I am no longer a slave to sin but a slave to righteousness through Jesus Christ. I receive your grace to change. Let me operate from a pure heart and I will see your magnificence manifest in my life. In the mighty name of Jesus, I pray! Amen.

I am encouraged! You be encouraged, too!

Day 67

Holy Spirit Prayers

Psalm 141:2 KJV

Let my prayer be set forth before thee as incense; and the lifting up of my hands as the evening sacrifice.

Psalm 6:9 KJV

The Lord hath heard my supplication; the Lord will receive my prayer.

Romans 8:26 KJV

Likewise the Spirit also helpeth our infirmities: for we know not what we should pray for as we ought: but the Spirit itself maketh intercession for us with groanings which cannot be uttered.

Grace and Peace, Beloved!

How wonderful it is that we do not need to pray in our own strength! The Holy Spirit is here to intercede on our behalf and pray perfect prayers through us as we yield our tongues to speak heaven's language. He is here to help us navigate life. We can depend on Him.

As you pray the prayer below, know that I am agreeing with you. I am praying for every heart crying out to know the Father better. As we draw close to the Father, he draws close to us.

Today's Prayer:

Father, thank your for sending me the Comforter, the Holy Spirit, to help me navigate life. Holy Spirit, I need you; I need your power. As I pray today, receive my prayers as a sweet incense, a fragrant offering, to you. As I study your word today and in the upcoming days, bring the scriptures to life for me; help me to apply the word in a practical way. I pray that the light of Jesus shines brightly in and through me so that others see you. Open my spiritual ears and spiritual eyes that I may discern and access the hidden treasures stored up for me. I receive your rest and your peace. In the mighty name of Jesus, I pray! Amen.

I am encouraged! You be encouraged, too!

Day 68

Prayer for Guidance in Ministry

Acts 1:8 KJV

But ye shall receive power, after that the Holy Ghost is come upon you: and ye shall be witnesses unto me both in Jerusalem, and in all Judaea, and in Samaria, and unto the uttermost part of the earth.

Acts 10:38 KJV

How God anointed Jesus of Nazareth with the Holy Ghost and with power: who went about doing good, and healing all that were oppressed of the devil; for God was with him.

2 Timothy 1:7 KJV

For God hath not given us the spirit of fear; but of power, and of love, and of a sound mind.

Grace and Peace, Beloved!

We live in a critical period and it is important that we, as believers, activate our power or put our good skills to use, so to speak. It is our responsibility as children of the King to assist others in breaking free from

166

satan's grasp. By the power of the Holy Spirit and the blood of Jesus, we are able to do good and heal all who are oppressed of the devil.

Spiritual warfare is real. We wear our armor according to Ephesians 6 to stand against the devices of satan. Mind you, our combat is not with flesh and blood but against spiritual forces of darkness that have blinded the minds of many people in this hour. Jesus Christ has obtained our victory through his precious blood. Hence, we are victorious; we are triumphant against evil.

I challenge you this week to Ask, Seek, Knock. *Ask* the Holy Spirit how you can minister to someone, *seek* an opportunity to do so, and *knock* on the doors of that person's heart to share the good news of the Kingdom. Our life of righteousness, peace, and joy is a life of action as the Holy Spirit leads. We live, move, and have our being in God. Activate your power!

Today's Prayer:

Father, I thank you that you have chosen me to live in this time period. You are extremely purposeful, and I know that it is your divine plan that I be alive in this moment to advance your Kingdom. I yield to you, Holy Spirit, to reveal to me that person or those persons to whom I can minister this week. You are preparing their hearts as well as mine for an encounter with you. Thank you, Father, that your love is available to all. I cast aside any doubt or fear and rely on your strength as I follow your direction. In the mighty name of Jesus, I pray! Amen.

I am encouraged! You be encouraged, too!

Day 69

Prayer of Agreement

Matthew 18:19-20 KJV

19 Again I say unto you, That if two of you shall agree on earth as touching any thing that they shall ask, it shall be done for them of my Father which is in heaven.
20 For where two or three are gathered together in my name, there am I in the midst of them.

Romans 8:28 KJV

And we know that all things work together for good to them that love God, to them who are the called according to his purpose.

Romans 12:10 KJV

Be kindly affectioned one to another with brotherly love; in honour preferring one another;

Philippians 2:4 NKJV

Let each of you look out not only for his own interests, but also for the interests of others.

Grace and Peace, Beloved!

Are you struggling? Are you facing a problem that may seem insurmountable? Trust that God knows what you are going through and has your best interest at heart. As you rest in that truth, shift your focus. I urge you today to lay aside your issue; instead, focus on a brother or sister who needs your prayer support. As the scripture admonishes, consider the interests of others.

Life is not a funfair; it's a warfare. Life is not always a walk in the park; we know that tests will come. However, prayer is our weapon. Commit to agree in prayer for the breakthrough of someone else. Since the battle belongs to God, both you and your friend are victorious.

Today's Prayer: (As you pray, insert your friend's name in the blank).

Father, I thank you for good relationships and strong friendships. I agree in prayer today with my friend, _____. Your word speaks of true friends who stick closer than our relatives. Help me, Holy Spirit, to be that type of friend. _____ is experiencing pain, and I count this situation as an invitation to pray. Lord, give _____ the wisdom, the courage, and the strength to endure until deliverance manifests. I bind the activity of satan from around my friend, and I release your righteousness, peace, and joy in the Holy Spirit. I release angels, mighty warriors, to assist my friend in this time of need. Thank you, Father. I declare that all is well with my friend and his/her household. In the mighty name of Jesus, I pray! Amen.

I am encouraged! You be encouraged, too!

Day 70

Intense Prayer in the Time of Battle

1 Timothy 2:1 VOICE

So, first and foremost, I urge God's people to pray. They should make their requests, petitions, and thanksgivings on behalf of all humanity.

Jude 20 KJV

But ye, beloved, building up yourselves on your most holy faith, praying in the Holy Ghost,

Matthew 26:41 KJV

Watch and pray, that ye enter not into temptation: the spirit indeed is willing, but the flesh is weak.

Grace and Peace, Beloved!

Prayer is vital. It is so powerful that it changes natural circumstances. We are to enforce our Kingdom authority by watching and praying. Let us be proactive. Instead of waiting for the storm to awaken us or waiting for attacks of the enemy to start praying, let us shift into Kingdom prayer mode now. Release the power of God by praying the word, praying in heaven's language, and listening for instructions.

The scriptures tell us that "the spirit is willing but the flesh is weak." In our hearts and minds, we desire to do right, but because of this fallen world we live in, our natural bodies will operate contrary to God's righteous path for our lives. Through prayer, we strengthen our spirit man and support our own spiritual growth. In effect, we position our spirit man to tell our flesh what to do. In other words, we get our flesh under control. Prayer is for our own good, Beloved!

As you pray today and in the days to come, expect your sensitivity to spiritual activity to increase. Expect your discernment to be heightened. You will begin to immediately recognize satan's attacks and stop them with the word of God. Now release the blessing of God over your life and the lives of your loved ones.

Today's Prayer:

Father, I thank you for the courage to pray big, bold prayers. I am a student of your word and wield prayer as my weapon. Your word is sharp and able to cut the enemy off immediately. I thank you for being involved in my prayer time – for listening and speaking to me. My prayers are productive. In the mighty name of Jesus, I pray! Amen.

I am encouraged! You be encouraged, too!

Day 71

Listen and Live

Psalm 42:1 KJV

As the hart panteth after the water brooks,
so panteth my soul after thee, O God.

Isaiah 55:3 NIV

3 Give ear and come to me; listen, that you may live.   I will make an
everlasting covenant with you, my faithful love promised to David.

Psalm 46:10 KJV

Be still, and know that I am God:
I will be exalted among the heathen, I will be exalted in the earth.

Grace and Peace, Beloved!

We have all heard this statement in some variation, "You can't get a word in edgewise." We know what that means. A one-sided conversation (which is really no conversation at all) is on display. In the context of prayer, too often we forget the importance of listening. Communing with our Father is a dialogue. We are in communication with each other and in intimate fellowship. I love the connection in Isaiah 55:3 (NIV) – listen and live.

After you pray the prayer below, take whatever time you need to be silent and hear the Father's answers. You will be amazed at his response as you intentionally listen.

Today's Prayer:

Father, let me hear the beating of your heart today. In my still time, let me hear your voice clearly. Let me listen for what pleases you. I want to be in alignment with you so that your glory can be seen in my life. I want to know what is important to you. I want to hate the things you hate and to love the things you love. I believe you are guiding my heart and I wait quietly to hear your voice. In the mighty name of Jesus, I pray! Amen.

I am encouraged! You be encouraged, too!

Part 10
Thanksgiving
&
Praise

Day 72

An Attitude of Gratitude

1 Thessalonians 5:18 KJV

In every thing give thanks: for this is the will of God in Christ Jesus concerning you.

Psalm 136:1 KJV

O give thanks unto the Lord; for he is good:
for his mercy endureth for ever.

Philippians 4:6-7 KJV

6 Be careful for nothing; but in every thing by prayer and supplication with thanksgiving
let your requests be made known unto God.
7 And the peace of God, which passeth all understanding, shall keep your hearts and minds through Christ Jesus.

Grace and Peace, Beloved!

Let thanksgiving be in our hearts and in our mouths. Thanksgiving brings peace to our hearts. There are so many blessings for which we can be thankful.

I will make this personal. Let me start with the reasons I am thankful. I am thankful for sweet sleep, sweet rest, and for the Father waking me up this morning. I am thankful for my health and for food to eat. I am thankful for Christ paying the ultimate sacrifice for the forgiveness of my sin, taking the punishment for my sin, and restoring me back to right standing with the Father. The Father sent Jesus to die for my redemption, and Jesus yielded to the Father's will. Oh, if it were not for the Father's grace and mercy, where would I be?

In what ways and for what reasons are you thankful? Let me ask this differently. Has the Lord done anything for which you should be grateful? Have you seen God move and act on your behalf?

Ponder on those questions today and set your thermostat on gratitude.

Today's Prayer:

Father, I am grateful to you. Jesus, I thank you. Holy Spirit, I thank you. I will not allow my heart to be ungrateful nor my mouth to agree with the enemy by complaining. Help me to always be thankful for thankfulness is your will. In the mighty name of Jesus, I pray! Amen.

I am encouraged! You be encouraged, too!

Day 73

Thank Him in Advance

Numbers 23:19 KJV

God is not a man, that he should lie; neither the son of man, that he should repent: hath he said, and shall he not do it? or hath he spoken, and shall he not make it good?

Psalm 23:5 KJV

Thou preparest a table before me in the presence of mine enemies: thou anointest my head with oil; my cup runneth over.

Romans 4:20-21 KJV

20 He staggered not at the promise of God through unbelief; but was strong in faith, giving glory to God; 21 and being fully persuaded that, what he had promised, he was able also to perform.

Grace and Peace, Beloved!

The integrity of God spurs us to thank him in advance. He is truth and does exactly what he says he will do. As we read Numbers 23:19 KJV, we see that God makes good on all his promises. He does not lie; he cannot lie. He is a God of integrity.

You may ask me why I can thank him in advance. You may ask me why I have such faith when I cannot see the natural manifestation of my prayers. Here is the reason. I am fully persuaded that God honors his word. I know who my God is and all that he is! I know he hears all my closet prayers. I have learned to pray not only for his hand but for his heart. So I praise and thank him in advance.

Meditate on this, Beloved! God is with you wherever you go. He has already gone before you and leveled every mountain. He has prepared people's hearts to welcome and assist you. He has prepared a table of abundance for you where you partake liberally in the presence of your enemies. In fact, he has made your enemies to be at peace with you.

Today's Prayer:

Father, I thank you for the spiritual eyes to see that you have my future. You are in front of me and behind me, leading me and guarding me. I reject any ill words spoken about me. I am forever grateful for your grace that has empowered me to live in your liberty. I thank you in advance for supernatural breakthroughs. In the mighty name of Jesus, I pray! Amen.

I am encouraged! You be encouraged, too!

179

Day 74

The Garment of Praise

Isaiah 61:3 KJV

To appoint unto them that mourn in Zion, to give unto them beauty for ashes, the oil of joy for mourning, the garment of praise for the spirit of heaviness; that they might be called trees of righteousness, the planting of the Lord, that he might be glorified.

Philippians 4:8 NIV

Finally, brothers and sisters, whatever is true, whatever is noble, whatever is right, whatever is pure, whatever is lovely, whatever is admirable—if anything is excellent or praiseworthy—think about such things.

Psalm 22:3 KJV

But thou art holy, O thou that inhabitest the praises of Israel.

Psalm 30:11 KJV

Thou hast turned for me my mourning into dancing: thou hast put off my sackcloth, and girded me with gladness;

Grace and Peace, Beloved!

We understand how a garment, essentially an article of clothing, is designed to protect us from outside elements. We wear slacks, shirts, undergarments, sweaters, coats, dresses, and the like for covering and to serve as a barrier against unwanted abrasion or contact with detrimental materials. Note that in Genesis 3:7 (KJV), Adam and Eve stitched garments from fig leaves; but in Genesis 3:21 (KJV), God provided Adam and Eve with better garments of skin or leather. God provided those garments as a better means of protection.

Garments can also signify economic status, ethnicity, spiritual order (as in the priest of the Old Testament, Exodus 35:19 KJV), special favor (as in Joseph's coat of many colors, Genesis 37:3 KJV), or royalty. Given that our Father is very strategic, I love that we have the reference to the "garment of praise" in Isaiah 61 (KJV).

Our Father promises us the better garment, one of high spiritual order and royal designation. Our Father desires that we exchange the spirit of heaviness for this royal garment. The heavy spirit tries to keep us from receiving the joy and peace that we have in Christ Jesus! This spirit is not of our Father but from the enemy. Anything heavy contradicts the words of Jesus, "For my yoke is easy, and my burden is light" (Matthew 11:30 KJV).

I am a witness of how satan (the hunter of souls) can harass us with this entangling spirit that is trying to continuously drain our minds and conflict our souls. God has given us the remedy! We belong to Jesus, and we don't have to accept the enemy's heaviness!

Remember, any heaviness that tries to come upon you is illegal and is trespassing. Meditate on the noble thoughts outlined in Philippians 4:8 (KJV). You are in control of your thoughts. You are an overcomer!

181

Today's Prayer:

Father, I will myself to think on you, your promises, and things that are admirable and praiseworthy. I do not walk weighted down, but I walk in the Spirit. I am rooted and grounded in your love. I receive the spirit of praise that you have promised. When I look back and see where you have brought me from, praise bursts forth. I know you are real in my life, and your living word leaps from the pages into my heart. Faith arises strongly in me! Thank you that my life prospers as my soul prospers; my joy is full and complete. In the mighty name of Jesus, I pray! Amen.

I am encouraged! You be encouraged, too!

Day 75

Praise as a Weapon

2 Chronicles 20:22 KJV

And when they began to sing and to praise, the LORD set ambushments against the children of Ammon, Moab, and mount Seir, which were come against Judah; and they were smitten.

Acts 16:25-26 KJV

25 And at midnight Paul and Silas prayed, and sang praises unto God: and the prisoners heard them.

26 And suddenly there was a great earthquake, so that the foundations of the prison were shaken: and immediately all the doors were opened, and every one's bands were loosed.

Psalm 18:3 KJV

I will call upon the LORD, who is worthy to be praised: So shall I be saved from mine enemies.

Grace and Peace, Beloved!

Our praise is a powerful weapon! Help is made available through our praise as we seek the Lord's face. Angels are assigned and released to break chains at the utterance of God's word. The account of Paul and Silas being released from prison underscores the chain-breaking, band-loosing power of praise. Engage your praise weapon to see changes in your life.

I have witnessed life transformation as I praise God at all times. I have learned that when God closes one door, he opens another. May your day be filled with spontaneous praise!

Today's Prayer:

Father, thank you for the weapon of praise. You inhabit my praises which are continually in my mouth. I deploy angels to guard, defend, and protect me and my household. Those angels, ministering spirits, are all around me. My life is transformed as I yield to you; I see miracles, signs, and wonders. In the mighty name of Jesus, I pray! Amen.

I am encouraged! You be encouraged, too!

Day 76

Praise Through the Valley

Psalm 23:4 KJV

*Yea, though I walk through the valley of the shadow of death, I will
fear no evil:
for thou art with me; thy rod and thy staff they comfort me.*

1 Timothy 1:18-19 VOICE

*18 Timothy, my dear child, I am placing before you a charge for the
mission ahead. It is in total agreement with the prophecies once spoken
over you. Here it is: with God's message stirring and directing you,
fight the good fight,
19 armed with faith and a good conscience. Some have tried to silence
their consciences, wrecking their lives and ruining their faiths.*

Exodus 33:14 KJV

And he said, My presence shall go with thee, and I will give thee rest.

Grace and Peace, Beloved!

We are in a good fight. A good fight means that we win. We win because we are on the Lord's side. He has equipped us with supernatural weapons. The word of God is our weapon; it is a sword.

Our praise and worship is also our weapon. Sometimes we suffer more in our imaginary thoughts than in reality! We have the anointing, the ability, and the capacity to destroy every thought that is contrary to the word of God.

I have found such peace in resting in God's word. It brings healing to my life. I place a demand on the healing virtue of Jesus just like the woman who had been bleeding for twelve years. My faith makes me whole (see Luke 8:43-48 and Mark 5:25-34).

Psalm 23 speaks of walking through the valley. Pay attention to the word "through." That word implies that you will arrive at the other side. Know that, in the valley, God is strengthening you and is with you, causing you to fear nothing. There are times when God delivers out of situations and times when he delivers through. In either case, you are always delivered because Jesus completed that work through his sacrifice. He believes in you! Run to the Living Word! Run to Jesus! Rely on him. Believe the word. Be a doer of the word and not simply a hearer. When you truly believe, corresponding action will follow. Engage your weapons. It's all good!

Today's Prayer:

Father, thank you for being dependable. I fret about nothing. With the word of God, I demolish every thought that is contrary to your perfect plan for my life. Praise and prayer are on my lips. I praise my way through. I extol you! Thank you, Jesus, for rescuing me and translating me into your Kingdom. I live well. In the mighty name of Jesus, I pray! Amen.

I am encouraged! You be encouraged, too!

Part 11
Trust, Rest,
&
Peace

Day 77

Trust Him for Guidance

Jeremiah 17:7-8 KJV

7 Blessed is the man that trusteth in the Lord,
and whose hope the Lord is.
8 For he shall be as a tree planted by the waters, and that spreadeth
out her roots by the river, and shall not see when heat cometh,
but her leaf shall be green; and shall not be careful in the year of
drought, neither shall cease from yielding fruit.

Psalm 138:8 KJV

The LORD will perfect that which concerneth me:
thy mercy, O LORD, endureth for ever:
forsake not the works of thine own hands.

Proverbs 12:28 KJV

In the way of righteousness is life: and in the pathway thereof there is
no death.

Grace and Peace, Beloved!

We are nothing without the Lord. We need Him every hour, every minute, and every second of our day. Yes, we need Him; yet, on the other side of our need, is the Lord's continual fulfilling of that need. He is always with us just as he said he would be. He satisfies fully and completely. We have an amazing assurance that there is a divine supply to meet our every need.

I am speaking to myself! I am reminding myself that the Father is concerned about everything about which I am concerned. Little things, big things, things that may seem insignificant to others, things that make me cry when I am alone, memories that need healing, misplacing my keys, my finances, my diet – it doesn't matter. My Father is responsible for my care. I acknowledge him today, in all my ways. I trust that he is directing me along his path for my life.

Today's Prayer:

Father, help me to simply trust and obey. I leave the consequences up to you. My desire is to do things your way. Your way is right, and you know what is best for me. Holy Spirit, go before me today and clear every path. In the mighty name of Jesus, I pray! Amen.

I am encouraged! You be encouraged, too!

Day 78

Stretch Your Trust

Psalm 13:5 KJV

But I have trusted in thy mercy; my heart shall rejoice in thy salvation.

I Corinthians 13:9-10 KJV

9 or we know in part, and we prophesy in part.
10 But when that which is perfect is come, then that which is in part shall be done away.

2 Corinthians 4:8-9 KJV

8 We are troubled on every side, yet not distressed; we are perplexed, but not in despair;
9 Persecuted, but not forsaken; cast down, but not destroyed;

Grace and Peace, Beloved!

No matter how big the problem is in our lives, all God wants us to do is TRUST! We serve a big God who knows all and sees all. We know him intimately. Again, he knows all. We, on the other hand, understand things in part not fully grasping the impact of our journey across generations. We do not need to know everything; we simply trust. So when we are perplexed by a mystery in our lives, that is the opportune time to get excited and draw close to the one who knows it all.

I encourage you to trust God, Beloved, and keep doing the right things. Look for an opportunity to stretch your trust, stretch your belief, stretch your faith. Relax in him and you will reap in due time.

Today's Prayer:

Father, show me how to stretch my trust in a practical way. I am going to another level in you. I can trust you with my life because you know things about me that I don't know. You see my past, present, and future. You look ahead and know every pitfall that I need to avoid. Thank you, Father, for being trustworthy and doing exactly what you say you will do. I trust you. In the mighty name of Jesus, I pray! Amen.

I am encouraged! You be encouraged, too!

Day 79

Navigating Difficult Decisions

Proverbs 3:5-6 KJV

5 Trust in the Lord with all thine heart;

and lean not unto thine own understanding.

6 In all thy ways acknowledge him, and he shall direct thy paths.

Habakkuk 3:19 AMPC

The Lord God is my Strength, my personal bravery, and my

invincible army; He makes my feet like hinds' feet and will make me to

walk [not to stand still in terror, but to walk] and make [spiritual] progress

upon my high places [of trouble, suffering, or responsibility]!

Isaiah 30:21 NKJV

Your ears shall hear a word behind you, saying,

"This is the way, walk in it," Whenever you turn to the right hand Or

whenever you turn to the left.

John 10:5, 27 KJV

5 And a stranger will they not follow, but will flee from him: for they know not the voice of strangers.

27 My sheep hear my voice, and I know them, and they follow me:

Grace and Peace, Beloved!

Life is full of decisions with some more difficult than others. God never wants us to remain immobile and fearful that we might make the wrong decision. No, no more fear, Beloved! As we trust him and follow him, we will make the right choices. The Holy Spirit is always right. God's word is clear about following his instructions to remain in the center of his will. Let us cooperate with our loving Father who has foreknowledge of what lies ahead. He is always looking out for our best interests.

As I share "real talk," I am being open about how trusting the Father plays out in my life. Each day, I face new choices, and I'm not always sure of what to do. Sometimes I feel paralyzed by having so many options, and I wonder if there really is only one that's right for me. I find value in praying until I have peace about my decisions.

My favorite verse is Proverbs 3:5,6 as noted as part of today's devotional. Trusting and obeying God has always put me in the center of his will – the exact place where I want to be.

Stretch your trust today, Beloved. Understand that following God will often not make sense in the natural. His instructions may not seem logical or based on the world's way of operating. It is okay. Trust, rest, and follow.

195

Today's Prayer:

Lord, as I make difficult decisions, help me to seek your wisdom by reading your word and asking for your guidance in prayer. As I experience your peace in prayer, I know that you are leading me. You are first in my life. Your instructions always keep me on the righteous path. Obeying you is always right. I trust, rest, and follow. In the mighty name of Jesus, I pray! Amen.

I am encouraged! You be encouraged, too!

Day 80

Supernatural Peace

Romans 8:28 KJV

And we know that all things work together for good
to them that love God,
to them who are the called according to his purpose.

Isaiah 26:3 KJV

Thou wilt keep him in perfect peace, whose mind is stayed on thee:
because he trusteth in thee.

Philippians 1:2 TPT

May the blessings of divine grace and supernatural peace that flow
from God our wonderful Father, and our Messiah, the Lord Jesus, be
upon your lives.

Grace and Peace, Beloved!

Say this with me- ALL THINGS. Just saying the words is powerful. I sense my atmosphere responding to the authority that Christ has given me to speak God's will into my life. All things includes sickness, health, poverty, riches, good, bad, ups, downs, and anything we can name across this spectrum of life. We see the use of presence tense in Romans 8:28 (KJV) - "all things **work** together for good." Faith is always now and no matter what we are facing, all things are actively working right now on our behalf and to our benefit towards our successful outcome.

From a very practical standpoint, how would this look for you? It could be that all hell is breaking loose in your life, and it seems like satan is destroying your family. Say ALL THINGS. It could be that your best friend is speaking negative words about you. Say ALL THINGS. Are your children being rebellious? ALL THINGS.

Encourage yourself. There is full restoration and healing in our obedience. If you are feeling downhearted, talk to yourself aloud. Tell yourself that you **know**, not think, but that you **know** all things work together for your good. A knowing comes from deep within your recreated spirit and from intimate fellowship with the Father. Now, expect his supernatural peace to reign supreme in your life.

Today's Prayer:

Father, thank you for your trustworthiness. I know that all things work together for my good, and I rest in that reassurance now. I expect to see your goodness today, Father, in the land of the living. I command every storm in my life to be still, and I release your joy, your strength, and supernatural peace over my life. I receive your full restoration, your healing, but most importantly your limitless love. Not only am I a recipient of your peace, but I carry your peace with me everywhere I go. All is well with me. In the mighty name of Jesus, I pray! Amen.

I am encouraged! You be encouraged, too!

Day 81

Supernatural Rest

Matthew 11:28-30 **MSG**

28 Are you tired? Worn out? Burned out on religion? Come to me.
Get away with me and you'll recover your life.
I'll show you how to take a real rest.
29 Walk with me and work with me—watch how I do it.
Learn the unforced rhythms of grace.
30 I won't lay anything heavy or ill-fitting on you.
Keep company with me and you'll learn to live freely and lightly.

Psalm 116:7 **KJV**

Return unto thy rest, O my soul; for the Lord hath dealt bountifully
with thee.

1 Peter 5:7 **NIV**

Cast all your anxiety on him because he cares for you.

Jeremiah 31:25 **MSG**

I'll refresh tired bodies; I'll restore tired souls.

Grace and Peace, Beloved!

What a relief it is to know that Jesus is ready to receive all of our cares, anxieties, and worries. He is always there to refresh and strengthen us. When we are exhausted, he is right there. When we feel overwhelmed, he is there. Jesus is so good to us that he anticipated those times of burn out. The remedy is to get away with him to rest.

On a personal note, I have experienced days of complete exhaustion. There have been times where I was stressed out emotionally, physically, and spiritually. I found myself wishing that everything would just stop for a few hours so that I could rest. Of course, the world did not stop. I knew I had to enter his presence. My peace depended on it. He was there for me and always will be.

Beloved, remember that Jesus centers your life. Create a space to be still. Sit in his presence. You will be refreshed and able to think clearly as you sort out your priorities. It is okay to take a timeout.

Today's Prayer:

Father, forgive me for neglecting my time with you. I bask in your peace, protection, and love. As you promised, order my steps today. Help me to focus on the promises in your word. Remembering who you are calms my clamoring thoughts. I need your guidance in all things. I receive your supernatural rest today. In the mighty name of Jesus, I pray! Amen.

I am encouraged! You be encouraged, too!

Part 12
Beyond the Book

Day 82

Continual Revelation

3 John 2 KJV

Beloved, I wish above all things that thou mayest prosper and be in health, even as thy soul prospereth.

Proverbs 4:7 KJV

Wisdom is the principal thing; therefore get wisdom: and with all thy getting get understanding.

Ephesians 1:3 KJV

Blessed be the God and Father of our Lord Jesus Christ, who hath blessed us with all spiritual blessings in heavenly places in Christ:

Grace and Peace, Beloved!

The anointing of Jesus Christ is upon us to prosper in every area of our lives. We will prosper and be in health in the proportion and according to how our soul prospers. As we read the scriptures, it is important that we understand what we are reading. The Holy Spirit will reveal his meaning as we submit to him. The Father has already blessed us. All we need do is receive.

During your personal time of reading and study, make a decision to interact with what you read. Ask the Holy Spirit to reveal meaning and ways in which you can apply the scriptures to your life daily. May your heart forever be postured to receive mercy; may goodness follow you throughout your day! Look for them, Beloved!

Today's Prayer:

Father, I bless your Holy Name! I worship you forever. I am so grateful that you have already blessed me and seated me together with Jesus at your right hand. I receive your goodness and mercy for my life. I prosper in all that I do. In the mighty name of Jesus, I pray! Amen.

I am encouraged! You be encouraged, too!

Day 83

Always Seek Him

Matthew 7:7-8 KJV

7 Ask, and it shall be given you; seek, and ye shall find; knock, and it shall be opened unto you:
8 For every one that asketh receiveth; and he that seeketh findeth; and to him that knocketh it shall be opened.

Proverbs 8:17 KJV

I love them that love me; and those that seek me early shall find me.

Jeremiah 29:13 KJV

And ye shall seek me, and find me,
when ye shall search for me with all your heart.

Grace and Peace, Beloved!

Today is a good day, a grand day to be alive. Father has a perfect plan for our lives and a perfect plan for this day. You know, the enemy attempts to distract us with idols which may take many forms. An idol for one person may be preoccupation with social media while another may be people pleasing while, yet another, may be meditating on the enemy's lies, in other words worrying.

Allow God to be first in your heart and dismiss any idol that tries to preempt your intimacy with the Father. Seek his course for today. Ask him boldly, and he will reveal all the good that is in store for you.

Today's Prayer:

Father, I walk in increased intimacy with you. Reveal to me all that you want me to do and every step I should take. I am seeking you because you know me better than I know myself. I reject the lies of the enemy that I am incapable or insignificant. Instead, I agree with the will of Christ to give me abundant life. Before you formed me in my mother's womb, you called me, chose me, and predestined me to by your child. I allow my life to conform to your word about me. I expect goodness and mercy to show up and show out today. In the mighty name of Jesus, I pray! Amen.

I am encouraged! You be encouraged, too!

Day 84

The Father is Our Priority

Matthew 6:33 KJV

But seek ye first the kingdom of God, and his righteousness;
and all these things shall be added unto you.

1 Kings 17:13 KJV

And Elijah said unto her, Fear not; go and do as thou hast said:
but make me thereof a little cake first, and bring it unto me,
and after make for thee and for thy son.

Luke 12:31 KJV

But rather seek ye the kingdom of God;
and all these things shall be added unto you.

Grace and Peace, Beloved!

There is such a blessing on the other side of putting God first. Putting God first is imperative. Doors and windows of opportunity will open when we give God the honor of first place in our lives. I love the story of the widow of Zarephath in 1 Kings 17. During a time of drought, the widow obeyed the prophet Elijah and prepared a meal for him first out of her meager supply. After feeding Elijah first, miraculously, her flour and oil were supernaturally multiplied.

That is how the Kingdom works. In the books of Matthew and Luke, we read Jesus' instructions to seek the Kingdom first. When we put God first, we position ourselves to hear from him and receive his abundance.

This way of putting God first can be expressed in many ways. If we want our marriage to prosper, we need his wisdom. So we put him first! As we honor God's sacred place in our lives, we will discover that everything concerning our careers, education, health, family, relationships, decisions, and finances falls into place. So who would not want that? We need the Father's direction and correction in everything that we do. Jesus is the Anointed One who sets us apart and makes our lives different from the world. In fact, Colossians 1:18 (KJV) speaks of the "preeminence" of Christ, meaning he is first in all things.

I encourage you to evaluate your life, your schedule, and your priorities today. Determine if there are any areas where you have not honored God as first place in your life. It is very simple to change course. Make the necessary adjustments and watch your life change for the better.

Today's Prayer:

Father, help me to put you first. Show me the practical ways in which I can put you first in my life. I know you are working in me to fulfill your highest purpose. I trust you to solidify the desire in me to put you first and help me to live it out. Thank you, Holy Spirit, for teaching me and showing me the way. I thank you, Father, for answering me. I honor and glorify you today. I am privileged to be your child. In the mighty name of Jesus, I pray! Amen.

I am encouraged! You be encouraged, too!

Day 85

Supernatural Wisdom and Insight

Psalm 119:18 KJV

Open thou mine eyes, that I may behold wondrous things
out of thy law.

Ephesians 1:18 KJV

The eyes of your understanding being enlightened; that ye may know
what is the hope of his calling, and what the riches of the glory of his
inheritance in the saints,

Psalm 119:105 KJV

Thy word is a lamp unto my feet, and a light unto my path.

Grace and Peace, Beloved!

Have you ever assisted someone with poor eyesight? If so, I am sure you were honored to assist; however, the simplest activities became more difficult due to the impairment. Think about the person who wears glasses. Choosing to not wear the glasses, the corrective lenses, while driving is likely to cause some type of mishap. So it is with us when we have not fed

211

ourselves with the word of God. Without the word, we are like a person with poor eyesight.

The word of God is here to direct us. When we look into the light of the word of God, we see our way clearly. Truths unfold as we rely on God's word. We see peace, mercy, grace, compassion, kindness, God's intense love, and the pure essence of God himself. We see the passion of Jesus Christ and how his great transaction transported us into his kingdom. Likewise, we see satan for who he is, a deceiver and the father of lies. Yes, the word of God reveals things to us.

As you walk with him, expect to have insight beyond your five senses. You will have wisdom beyond the parameters of your natural mind. God is sharpening your perception so that you live a victorious life.

Today's Prayer:

Father, thank you for revealing yourself to me through your word and my intimate time with you. I thirst for you, as a deer pants for water. Your word is a lamp to help guide me along your path of righteousness. I trust you to lead me. I receive your supernatural wisdom and insight. In the mighty name of Jesus, I pray! Amen.

I am encouraged! You be encouraged, too!

Day 86

Do Not Be Deceived

Matthew 5:48 KJV

Be ye therefore perfect, even as your Father
which is in heaven is perfect.

Revelation 12:9 KJV

And the great dragon was cast out, that old serpent, called the Devil,
and Satan, which deceiveth the whole world: he was cast out into the
earth, and his angels were cast out with him.

Titus 2:13 KJV

Looking for that blessed hope, and the glorious appearing of the great
God and our Saviour Jesus Christ;

Ephesians 5:11 VOICE

Don't get involved with the fruitless works of darkness; instead,
expose them to the light of God.

Grace and Peace, Beloved!

We have true hope in Christ Jesus. That blessed hope stirs our souls and keeps us moving forward. On the contrary, satan is the deceiver of the world. He raises false hope. One way he deludes is by placing distractions in our lives. When we allow the cares of this life and the glamour of riches to become priority in our lives, we have erected idols. These idols choke the word and our minds are deceived, blinded to the truth. Believers we must see! I am referring to spiritual sight. No, we are not perfect in our own abilities, but Christ has commanded us to be perfect meaning we are to mature and grow. Daily, we submit ourselves to the work of grace in order to be like him. The more we are like him, the less opportunity for us to be deceived.

Strengthen yourself in the knowledge of God, Beloved! Exercise in the things of the Spirit. Walk in the fruit of the Spirit! Truth is our defense. Spread the word and be a witness to the glory of God in your life. Walk in the light for the light has no communion with darkness.

Today's Prayer:

Father, I keep my focus on you. I am laser-focused on your love for me. I remove the distractions of which I am aware and ask you to remove distractions that I do not see. I am no longer focused on my problems because your love is enough. I am filled with your wisdom, knowledge, and understanding. I am hopeful about my future expecting your goodness and mercy to run me over. In the mighty name of Jesus, I pray! Amen.

I am encouraged! You be encouraged, too!

Day 87

Heart Meditations

Psalm 19:14 KJV

Let the words of my mouth, and the meditation of my heart, be acceptable in thy sight, O Lord, my strength, and my redeemer.

1 Peter 1:13 NIV

Therefore, with minds that are alert and fully sober, set your hope on the grace to be brought to you when Jesus Christ is revealed at his coming.

Psalm 1:1-3 KJV

1 Blessed is the man that walketh not in the counsel of the ungodly, nor standeth in the way of sinners, nor sitteth in the seat of the scornful.

2 But his delight is in the law of the Lord; and in his law doth he meditate day and night.

3 And he shall be like a tree planted by the rivers of water, that bringeth forth his fruit in his season; his leaf also shall not wither; and whatsoever he doeth shall prosper.

Grace and Peace, Beloved!

Let us remember that our almighty God cares for us. We are mindful of the word that tells us nothing will ever separate us from his love! That mindfulness could include meditation (keeping the word at the forefront of our thoughts), reading and proclaiming the word aloud, partaking in communion as we remember the magnitude of what Christ has done, or other methods of undistracted focus on the word of God. As we concentrate on God's truth, the word becomes big and strong in our spirits until we know for certain that nothing is powerful enough to disconnect us from the love of God! And for that, Father, we give you thanks!

Continue planting seeds of the word in your heart, Beloved! Also, water those seeds with the very same word. You will produce much fruit.

Today's Prayer:

Heavenly Father, your mercies are new every morning, and your faithfulness toward me is unmatched! Father, I understand that life will bring challenges, tests, and trials. In the midst of trials, I look to you. When I have doubts, help me to place my faith in you! I stir up my faith today. I place my hope in you. I sow the word of God in my heart so that I produce much fruit and prosper. In the mighty name of Jesus, I pray! Amen.

I am encouraged! You be encouraged, too!

Day 88

Our Blessed Hope

Matthew 24:31 KJV

*And he shall send his angels with a great sound of a trumpet, and they
shall gather together his elect from the four winds,
from one end of heaven to the other.*

John 8:12 KJV

*Then spake Jesus again unto them, saying, I am the light of the world:
he that followeth me shall not walk in darkness,
but shall have the light of life.*

Acts 17:28 KJV

*For in him we live, and move, and have our being; as certain also of
your own poets have said, For we are also his offspring.*

Psalm 149:4 NIV

*For the Lord takes delight in his people; he crowns the humble with
victory.*

Grace and Peace, Beloved!

We live for this moment. The day we'll hear the trumpet sound. We should be willing to die for our faith! In him we move, and live, and have our being. As we live out God's breath in this earth, let us BE who he called us to be. We are human BEings, not human DOings.

The Father is working his great plan for mankind through you and all the saints. Jesus has already prayed for you and the Father delights in you. He has ensured that you reach your destination.

Today's Prayer:

Father, thank you for sending your son, Jesus. Thank you for supercharging my heart with his light and life. The old me has died; I am a new creation in Christ Jesus. I will never be the same. You are my sustenance and the center of my joy. In the mighty name of Jesus, I pray! Amen.

I am encouraged! You be encouraged, too!

Day 89

Urgent Matters

1 Corinthians 15:52 KJV

In a moment, in the twinkling of an eye, at the last trump: for the trumpet shall sound, and the dead shall be raised incorruptible, and we shall be changed.

Colossians 3:3-4 KJV

*3 For ye are dead, and your life is hid with Christ in God.
4 When Christ, who is our life, shall appear, then shall ye also appear with him in glory.*

2 Peter 3:10 KJV

But the day of the Lord will come as a thief in the night; in the which the heavens shall pass away with a great noise, and the elements shall melt with fervent heat, the earth also and the works that are therein shall be burned up.

Luke 21:27 KJV

27 And then shall they see the Son of man coming in a cloud with power and great glory.

Grace and Peace, Beloved!

Real talk today. Our devotional today is deep, but it's real. It is time to wake up! It is time for us to be vigilant and be ready for the return of our Lord, King, and Savior. The Lord will appear in the twinkling of an eye, and we shall all take on our immortal bodies. Be ready and stay ready. The day of the Lord is near! All of the clues point to his imminent return. We will not be found asleep, totally oblivious to the signs of the times. The bible says he will return like a thief in the night. Will that be today? Tomorrow?

Live today as if it were your last. In all that you do, do it unto the Lord with all your might. Now is the time to do anything and everything the Father has commanded you to do. Keep the return of our Savior at the forefront of your mind, and live like today is the day.

Today's Prayer:

Father, help me to be vigilant and to live each day as if it were my last. I know that Jesus will return soon. I keep this truth at the forefront of my life. I live this life with no regret. I share this urgent message with others, particularly those who do not know you. In the mighty name of Jesus, I pray! Amen.

I am encouraged! You be encouraged, too!

Day 90

Salvation is Free

Matthew 9:36-38 KJV

36 But when he saw the multitudes, he was moved with compassion
on them, because they fainted, and were scattered abroad,
as sheep having no shepherd.
37 Then saith he unto his disciples, The harvest truly is plenteous,
but the labourers are few;
38 Pray ye therefore the Lord of the harvest, that he will send forth
labourers into his harvest.

Matthew 10:8 KJV

Heal the sick, cleanse the lepers, raise the dead, cast out devils: freely
ye have received, freely give.

1 Corinthians 3:9 NIV

For we are co-workers in God's service; you are God's field, God's
building.

Mark 16:15 KJV

And he said unto them, Go ye into all the world, and preach the gospel to every creature.

2 Peter 3:9 KJV

The Lord is not slack concerning his promise, as some men count slackness; but is longsuffering to us-ward, not willing that any should perish, but that all should come to repentance.

Grace and Peace, Beloved!

Thank you for allowing me to share my heart with you. As the Holy Spirit instructed, I have given to you that which I received freely. I beseech you to go beyond the book and share the gospel, this message of grace, with someone who is hurting. As believers, we are all ministers of reconciliation with a call to share the good news. God is very patient. He is waiting on sinners to come to Christ and believers to evangelize. Feel free to use the Prayer of Salvation below to lead someone to Christ.

Today's Prayer:

Father, I thank you that you chose me, outside of time, to be your ambassador. Show me the people with whom I can share the good news this week. My expectation is high and I know that you are orchestrating a divine connection between me and those people. I pray peace and protection over each one of them as our paths are being established. Holy Spirit, help me to be sensitive to your leading. Give me the words to say. I will speak as you instruct. I yield myself to you. In the mighty name of Jesus, I pray! Amen.

A Prayer of Salvation:

Father, I believe that Jesus died for my past, present, and future sins. I respond to your great love for me. I repent of my sin and follow you forward. Thank you, Jesus, for saving me.

I am encouraged! You be encouraged, too!

Acknowledgments

To God be the Glory for all he has done. I honor you, Father,

for your loving guidance throughout my entire life,

even in times when I felt you were not there.

Now I know that you have never left my side.

Thank you for the courage, the anointing, and the revelation to share

my story in this way for your glory.

To my friend and editor, Crystal L. Lee, for seeing my vision and

making my words blossom on the written page.

References

"delight." 2023. In *Merriam-Webster.com*. Merriam-Webster,

    Retrieved August 2, 2023, from https://www.merriam-

    webster.com/dictionary/delight. The Fragrant Garden.

Johansson, G. (2023). *20 Mind-blowing Mustard Tree Facts That*

    You Probably Didn't Know. https://thefragrantgarden.com/

    mustard-tree-facts/

"salvation." 2023. In *Merriam-Webster.com*. Merriam-Webster,

    Retrieved August 2, 2023, from https://www.merriam-

    webster.com/dictionary/salvation

Soroski, Jason. "What Does Shalom Mean & Why Is it

    Important?" *Crosswalk.com,* 3 Mar 2021,

    www.crosswalk.com/faith/spiritual-life/what-does-shalom-

    mean.html.

World Changers Church International. (2018, March 19). *We all*

    have a past, but we no longer live there. https://worldchangers.org/

    Daily-Devotionals/Weekly-Grace/We-All-Have-a-Past-but-We-

    No-Longer-Live-There

www.ingramcontent.com/pod-product-compliance
Lightning Source LLC
LaVergne TN
LVHW051728080426
835511LV00018B/2942